MISSION DRIVEN

MISSION DRIVEN

The Path *to a* Life *of* Purpose

MIKE HAYES

GRAND
CENTRAL

NEW YORK   BOSTON

Grand Central Publishing
Hachette Book Group
1290 Avenue of the Americas, New York, NY 10104
grandcentralpublishing.com
@grandcentralpub

First edition: September 2025

Grand Central Publishing is a division of Hachette Book Group, Inc. The Grand Central Publishing name and logo is a registered trademark of Hachette Book Group, Inc.

The publisher is not responsible for websites (or their content) that are not owned by the publisher.

Grand Central Publishing books may be purchased in bulk for business, educational, or promotional use. For information, please contact your local bookseller or the Hachette Book Group Special Markets Department at special.markets@hbgusa.com.

Library of Congress Cataloging-in-Publication Data has been applied for.
ISBNs: 9780306836510 (hardcover), 9780306836534 (ebook)

Printed in the United States of America

LSC-C

Printing 1, 2025

*To Ni and Maeson: No words can express
my profound love and appreciation.*

*To my fallen SEAL brothers and their Gold Star
families: I'm sorry and thank you. I will never forget.*

CONTENTS

AUTHOR'S NOTE

When I set out to write my first book, *Never Enough*, I had a very specific aim: I wanted to offer readers inspiration to live their greatest lives by sharing stories from the battlefield and the boardroom in the hope they would add up to the message that by focusing on excellence, agility, and meaning, you could achieve just about anything. I also wrote the book with the goal of earning money to pay off mortgages for Gold Star families—the spouses and children of brave teammates who died while fighting for our nation or by suicide post-combat.

With the help of readers like you, the 501(c)(3) nonprofit I founded, The 1162 Foundation, has paid off twelve Gold Star widows' mortgages to date, vastly improving the lives of those families and freeing those spouses and children to make their own impacts on the world. I've heard from so many readers who were motivated and moved by the book, but I've also heard from readers who were left with a more tactical question: *"I want to do more—I know I can do more—but how?"*

"How do I get," they ask me, *"from where I am now to a place where I am making a tangible difference for myself and for the world? How do I achieve what I'm hoping to, what I'm dreaming of, what I was put on this planet for?"*

"How do I make the greatest impact? And how do I wake up every morning excited to start the day, knowing that my work and my life are aligned with who I believe myself to be, who I want to be, and who I know I am?"

These are hard questions, and they're hard questions whether you are eighteen years old and looking for your first job, you're forty-five and contemplating what matters most in the decades ahead, you're sixty-seven and transitioning from a full-time role to what might be next for you, or you're ninety-nine and reflecting on your legacy. We are all in search of guidance, and it is almost surely the case that the most ambitious, most motivated, and most talented of us need guidance most of all. We all need guidance because we all have choices, in some form. Choices require choosing. And choosing is fraught, complicated, and difficult.

I don't have all the answers—and people who say they do are deluding themselves—but I do know that I've learned over the years a lot of the right questions to ask. I know of no one else who has served at my level in the military and the White House, and then made it to the C-suite in Fortune 500 corporate America. I've worked on the for-profit side at a number of outstanding companies, and on the non-profit side, helping to lead the largest museum fund-raising campaign in history as the founding board member for the National Medal of Honor Museum and through my own foundation. As a leader in both the finance and technology industries, I've interviewed, hired, and trained hundreds of individuals, and taught my teams how to nurture the rising stars that surround them. Between the public and the private sectors, I've worked with thousands of high achievers and helped guide many of them in shaping their careers, including counseling hundreds of SEALs—some of the most gifted, talented, ambitious individuals there are—looking for their next step after leaving the military. I've had college basketball and football stars call me for advice on whether they should leave school for the draft, and coaches ask me similar questions about whether to stay where they are or move to the next level. I've witnessed how some of the most accomplished organizations on the planet make their most critical decisions. I've learned from leaders, young and old, every step of the way.

Given all of that, when someone comes to me for advice, it's pretty easy to come up with what *I* would do in their situation. I've learned what's important to me, what moves me, what motivates me, what excites me, what skills I bring to the table, and what impacts I'm able to make on the people around me.

But what I would do, in someone else's shoes, does not matter, not even a little bit.

And that's where virtually all advice we typically receive runs aground. The best choices for me have no relevance unless they're also the best choices for you. Something one leader told me when I was talking him through his job search is that everyone was telling him what they thought he should do, but no one was asking him the questions to help him discover it for himself.

The only way to know the best choices for yourself is to start asking questions.

This is the book that asks those questions and operationalizes the conversations I have every day trying to help people make the right decisions for their lives. If you ask yourself the right questions and map every aspect of your life back to those answers, back to the kind of person you want to be and the life you want to live, then the choices become so much easier.

By diving deep into how we can each define success as individuals, and then providing tools for how to reach that success in our careers, in our lives, and for the world, this book is designed to help you discover *who* you want to be, and *what* you need to do to get there. I've written it in many respects so I can scale myself and make a positive impact on far more individuals than I'd ever be able to talk with one-on-one.

Whether you're just starting out, already an established leader, or in the midst of a transition and don't quite know how to figure out your next step, there is never a moment when digging deeper to ensure alignment with your core goals is a bad thing. My desire is to push you—and this book should force some serious thinking, and hopefully some hard work. I bring to the pages a bias in favor of action and of service, informed by my own battle-tested lens on human potential and the practical application of that potential in a wide range of fields. In short, while I've built up an arsenal of stories that I hope will provide inspiration along the way—whether from my own journey or the journeys of others I've contributed to or witnessed—this book is about so much more than inspiration. It's about a concrete framework I've been able to build from decades of leadership experience, aimed at *helping you personally find and achieve your mission.*

Are you ready to become Mission Driven and embark on a path to a life of purpose? If so, there's no time to waste.

INTRODUCTION

My friend John Gallagher is one of the most impressive people I know. He's a West Point graduate with two master's degrees who spent nearly thirty years in the Army. Along the way, as both an infantry commander and trusted adviser at the highest levels, he received just about every service award there is. A quiet force behind so many of our nation's prominent leaders—working on our toughest problems—John has served in two White House administrations and as an adviser to numerous four-star military commanders and senior defense officials whose names we would all recognize from the news. He is a principled leader with a strategic mind and strong faith, honored by seniors and subordinates—awarded the Legion of Merit, a Bronze Star for his service in Afghanistan, and the Presidential Service Badge, just to name a few. Perhaps most notably, he's been honored by his peers—without him realizing at the time that the people who knew him best were working in the background to make sure he received the recognition he deserved.

When I think about someone being Mission Driven, it's John.

And that mission is very clear: Every day, he is working to help our nation and inspire others to do the same, whether during his time in a military uniform, as a civilian leader in the public sector, or as a business executive in the private sector. It's why I nominated him for the White House Fellows Foundation & Association IMPACT Award in 2023, given annually to the White House Fellow alumnus who best demonstrates a lifetime spent contributing to society in transformational ways.

What is a White House Fellow? you may be wondering. The highly selective fellowship program was founded in 1964 by President Lyndon Johnson, to give young professionals—our country's future leaders—experience working at the highest levels of government and a view of how it all operates from the inside, while instilling in them a lifetime commitment to servant leadership. Fellows spend their time meeting with and learning from senior leaders, and taking on their own portfolios of great responsibility in an area of federal policy.

In my first book, *Never Enough: A Navy SEAL Commander on Living a Life of Excellence, Agility, and Meaning*, I wrote about the extraordinary privilege I felt to serve as a White House Fellow under Presidents George W. Bush and Barack Obama, and how the experience opened my eyes to what was possible. And what was possible wasn't just spending time in the Oval Office with the President or in the White House Situation Room helping to solve national crises, but also meeting people like John Gallagher, who were put on this planet to do exactly what they've spent their lives doing.

As John has served and led with distinction from the military to the private sector, I've been so proud of and excited for him, because he is such an incredible human being. There are few things better in life than seeing your friends succeed. And one of them is when you help make it happen.

I will never forget where I was when I got the call that John had won the IMPACT Award. I was so deeply moved to realize that, by nominating him, I had a role in this well-deserved honor. I knew how much John deserved it, and how much the award might increase his potential to go on and continue helping others for the rest of his life. The words of John's White House Fellow classmate, Brigadier General Bobbi Doorenbos, who introduced John at our annual gala for the award presentation, summed it up best: "John's brand of servant leadership is almost 'other-worldly' and comes from a place of absolute humility and selflessness. Superman wears John Gallagher pajamas."

As it happens, I'd previously nominated John for the award a year earlier, in 2022.

He didn't win.

Unbeknownst to me at the time, John had also nominated someone that year. John's nominee was the one who ended up winning.

It is not intended as a humblebrag to say that person was me. (And John might add that it was his superior nominating skills that made the difference!) It was a moving moment, no question, with a bit of a spiritual element to it. I was in the car when I found out, driving up to my lake house in New Hampshire, and as soon as I hung up the phone, I noticed there was just one other car on the road with me on Route 91, making our way through the stunningly beautiful Vermont mountains. I looked up and saw the license plate, a veterans' plate with a US flag on it—and the word BUMPA, which was the name I called my grandfather, my hero, my inspiration for everything. For me, it was unquestionably a sign from him, speaking directly to me: He was proud of me, and still watching over me every day—how else could I explain it?

But my win isn't the point. John's is, and there are two lessons I took from John's win, especially when I reflected back on my own. The first is that I was happier when John won than when I did, which is how I know I'm doing something right as a Mission Driven individual. The second is that it really is the journey and not the destination, because the truth is we are not changed by accolades and awards. I'm still the same, and John's still the same. The pleasure we feel is fleeting. It evaporates as quickly as it appears, and then we are left, once again, with ourselves and our own deeper reflections. If you are not driving toward something intrinsic in your being, heading every day toward fulfilling some larger mission that you care deeply about, then you will constantly be chasing the quick highs that will never pay off.

On the other hand, if you are motivated by a passion, a cause, a mission that belongs to you, your soul, and your spirit, then the quick highs don't matter. You feel at peace because you know you are meeting your purpose on this earth; you have a mission, and you are doing everything you can to achieve it.

The process of aligning our day-to-day selves with our mission in life is what I mean by Mission Driven, and helping you become Mission Driven is what this book is all about. No matter what it is in life that motivates you, some part of it must be expressed in how you spend your time each day—whether at work, outside of it, or ideally, in everything you do. I use the term *mission* and not *passion* intentionally, first because I don't think our passions should or will always align with every aspect of our lives, but more importantly, because a mission is bigger, more meaningful, and more directed to the world beyond ourselves. I firmly believe there is some component of each of us that is moved to make a difference—to improve the planet, the nation, or simply the people around us. We all have the innate sense that we're here to leave the world better than we found it, and to create a lasting legacy in some form. My aim with this book is to help you access your ability to contribute in the ways that best match your own gifts, strengths, interests, and desires. And when we, as individuals, can be Mission Driven, that's what makes us collectively stronger and better—as a community, as a country, and as a world. A win-win-win-win.

Some people will read that last paragraph and it will immediately click: Of course you want to make a difference, and you're ready for this book to help show you how. Others might be struggling with the whole concept: You want to succeed, and by that you mean you want to make money or get promoted...*so does this even apply to you?* I would argue it absolutely does, and for the sake of your own ultimate satisfaction, it absolutely must. It's great you want to make money; what do you want to do with it? It's great you want to provide for your family; what do you dream they will do when bolstered by the security you help to achieve for them? What are you trying to accomplish at the deepest level? What is a means to get you to your goal, and what is the end goal itself?

You don't need answers now, not to any of these questions; that's why you're reading this, and hopefully as you work your way through this book, you will get to know yourself a little better, and understand the desires that might still feel a little cloudy to you right now. Much of this book is driven by questions, rather than answers. My mission is likely not your mission; my gifts are not yours and your gifts are not mine; we all see the world differently. But that's the magic of community. Life would be dull if we were all the same, and much of our society would evaporate if we were all trying to achieve identical goals. We need people whose missions are to feed us, house us, draft our contracts, compose our soundtracks, fix our plumbing, and tell our stories.

And I should be very clear—for as much as it may appear that I have it all figured out, I haven't—and part of writing this book is about standing up and saying that people like me, who may superficially sound like they've won the game, are still struggling with the very same things that all of us struggle with each day. I've been as lost as anyone in my life, looking around and not sure what to do, facing challenging crossroads, leaning on great friends and mentors for direction and advice, and just trying to do my best to make the right decisions. Life is about helping each other understand that it's all okay, we're all human, and we're ultimately here to serve each other. The mission driving me—on the page and in my life—is to share, and to push us all to be a little less imperfect.

But how do we make the choices that get us to where we want to go?

And how do we ensure our choices are aligned with the lives we want to live, the people we want to be, and the impact we want to make?

Helping you find those answers is the *mission* of *Mission Driven*.

THE STRUCTURE OF THIS BOOK

Mission Driven is divided into two parts:

"The Long Game" focuses on *who* you want to be—as opposed to *what* you want to be. This means a deep dive into how you define success, and what kind of impact you're looking to have on the world. When you zoom out and think about a life well lived, the *what*s are temporary and transitory; the *who* provides the North Star for your entire being. Some people know their mission, and for them a big part of the journey is figuring out how to effectively translate dreams into successful lives and careers; others can't yet articulate their mission or may in some cases not have a mission that maps to an obvious professional pursuit—but there is *always* a way to craft a Mission Driven life. In all cases, you start with the person you want to be and then work backward to figure out how to achieve it—and the first five chapters of this book will provide the skills, exercises, and inspiration to do just that, uncovering your *who* and understanding the mindsets and practices that will help you live up to it at every stage of your life.

"The Short Game" then moves us from the *who* to the *how*, taking the learnings and discoveries you've gathered in "The Long Game" and applying them toward building your life, block by block. In the most practical sense, it's about finding your next great opportunities and making the best decisions as you do. The *who* intentionally comes first because so many people skip that step—and therefore, can't optimally solve for the *how*. Even more than that, too many people take a reactive, bottom-up approach to life, instead of looking top-down and starting with the person they want to be. Think about a typical job search, for instance: You hear about three jobs and spend your energy trying to decide which one is best, ignoring the universe of possibilities that happen not to have landed in your in-box. Instead of limiting our choices to the ones that are most easily seen by us, whether in a job search or otherwise, "The Short

Game" teaches how to proactively generate an expanded menu of opportunities that will lead to far greater reward, across all aspects of life—and ultimately enable us to give back and make a true impact on the world, in the ways we are driven to.

In both sections, we will toggle between stories, big-picture lessons, and exercises that will help you apply the points here to your own life. This is not just something to read; it's a guide to crafting your own Mission Driven path and truly changing your life.

CAN A BOOK *REALLY* CHANGE MY LIFE?

I'm not going to sugarcoat it. Some of the work you may need to do to become Mission Driven might be hard. On the one hand, you may be one of the fortunate ones whose mission is clear and whose path to get there is reasonably straightforward. You may find that luck smiles down upon you—though, truthfully, in most cases you make your own luck—and the ingredients for a Mission Driven life fall neatly into place.

For most of us, that's not the case—and that's especially true right now.

We live in a time when personal agency is more important than ever. Climbing the corporate ladder is no longer the career path for so many, and traditional definitions of "success" are being challenged by new generations and new technologies. Work and life flow together in ways they never did before—a fact that companies looking to win the war for talent have no choice but to recognize—and the right path to the lives we all want to live is often less obvious, less direct, and harder to navigate than we might have previously imagined. I talk to lots of executives who are preparing for a *plural* career, where you don't just have one operational role but do many things at once, and flow between multiple domains. So many of us are neither aiming for "normal" careers nor destined to follow them—and yet most advice hasn't caught up.

Many of the books I'm guessing you may have already read fail to appreciate the reality that inspiration, ambition, and yes, passion aren't enough; we all could benefit from concrete tips and step-by-step plans in order to manage the uncertainty around us. Professional and personal development in our constantly changing world is about agility. And if I've had to hone one trait through my range of experiences, it's agility. Agility, as it happens, is teachable. It's not always easy, but we all need to understand that moving and changing and pivoting aren't things you do once in a while, when you're forced to. They're things you do every day.

Because we are all at a transition point every single day.

And we never know for sure what's going to happen.

One more story before we jump in. John Connors (a different John than John Gallagher) was killed in action in December 1989, just months after he joined the SEALs. I was a freshman in college at Holy Cross at the time, participating in the Reserve Officers' Training Corps (ROTC) program but wrestling with what the right path in the Navy would be for me. John had graduated that past May from the Holy Cross ROTC unit, before I'd started college in the fall, so I never knew him.

There was a memorial service for John in St. Joseph's Chapel on the Holy Cross campus shortly after he died. It was mandatory for all the ROTC students to attend, and even though I had never met John, I found it indescribably moving to hear him eulogized. The words of his teammates and family about how he died protecting other SEALs under heavy enemy fire during a mission in Panama impressed upon me the enormous impact he had made in his short time in the SEALs and on the planet. John was just twenty-five years old when he died. The SEAL community was crushed by his and the other losses during that mission. And I saw how the SEALs came together as a community and how being a SEAL created an opportunity to make a real difference. That memorial service inspired me. John Connors changed my life.

I hadn't even considered the SEALs before John's memorial service. I didn't think I could hack it. I was a 170-pound freshman and could do maybe half a pull-up at that point. But three years later as a college senior needing to make a career decision, I decided I was going to do it. I was going to be a SEAL. (In the words of Yoda, there is no "try." Once you make a decision to do something, you do it.) After graduating from Basic Underwater Demolition/SEAL training (or "BUD/S") as one of 19 graduates from a class of 120, my first SEAL Team assignment turned out to be John's team, SEAL Team FOUR. I was one of the new guys there in 1994, the five-year anniversary of when John was killed in action. We held a memorial, and the executive officer, second in command of the Team, told us that John's family was also holding a service at Arlington National Cemetery, and asked if any of us wanted to attend.

I immediately volunteered. The officer assumed I had known John, but of course I hadn't. I merely figured I could be one more body in a show of support, wearing my dress uniform with the Navy SEAL trident and showing the family that there were more of us who cared.

John's legacy never left my memory.

And then, just a couple of years ago, I was asked to be a guest speaker at a fundraiser in Boston for a John Connors statue being built in his hometown of Scituate, Massachusetts, to honor the impact John had made in the world. It was hard for me to prepare that speech. I stepped up to the podium on a beautiful Boston night and looked out at the black-tie audience, 500 people strong, gathered at the USS *Constitution*—the oldest active naval vessel in the world. I told them I'd spent a lot of time thinking about what success is, and that one measure of success is if you can positively impact someone's life. I asked everyone to think about a person whose life they changed, and someone who changed theirs. We all remember conversations that moved our lives onto a different trajectory, that we reflect back on as turning points, times we are so glad we heard the words we did at the moment we heard them. I invited everyone to raise a hand if, as they thought back, they believed they'd ever truly impacted someone else's life. Of course, every hand went up.

"Amazing," I said. "Please put your hands down and celebrate yourself and your inspiring orientation to help others. It's what we need more of in this world and, in my opinion, the most important measure of success. But…it's not the highest level of that success," I continued. "Now raise your hand if you've ever changed the life of someone you *haven't met.*"

I could see everyone slightly puzzled—reflecting—*how do you even do that?* Not one hand went up. As I see it, even greater than impacting the lives of people you've taken the time to engage with is having the ability to impact the lives of people far beyond.

I looked straight at John's mother and siblings at the head table about twenty feet away, overwhelmed with emotion, working hard to hold it together. I said, at half speed, "Mrs. Connors, I never met John, but John changed my life."

I was at that podium speaking not because of what I'd achieved in life but because of John Connors and the impact he made on me—and surely countless others—whom he never even had the chance to know.

I will never have the chance to meet most of you, but my own measure of success for this book is how many lives it can impact, of strangers—and then, how many lives it can enable all of you to change as well. The cascading effect of lives changed for the better changes our world in profound and meaningful ways.

Because, as I said, every day is a transition point. We wake up every morning facing the choice to continue on the path we're already taking, or move to something new, embrace a different challenge, add, subtract, or shift the elements on our plates. We wake up every morning with the privilege to ask the big questions—and to answer them.

Is this the life I should be living?

Am I achieving all I should be?

Am I giving back? Am I making a difference? Am I happy?

Am I Mission Driven?

So, what's the verdict? Are *you* Mission Driven?

THE LONG GAME

CHAPTER ONE

Who, Not *What* You Want to Be

My very first job was as a dishwasher at the Newport Creamery, a beloved New England restaurant chain that for almost a century has been serving burgers, grilled cheese, and giant milkshakes that are impossible to resist (drink three and your fourth is free!). I was sixteen years old, earning $3.35 an hour, and all I wanted in the world was a car. I saw a 1982 Nissan Sentra for sale—canary yellow, $1400, and falling apart—and I did the math. If I worked all summer at the Creamery, I could earn just enough to buy the ride of my dreams.

The most experienced employee there was Bob, a forty-year-old who called himself "head dishwasher," and who'd been at the Creamery forever. Bob had big ambitions, and he loved to talk about them, but he also had some obvious limitations. He had intellectual disabilities, couldn't live on his own, and despite his desire, it was hard to see a path upward for him. Bob and I were at very different places in life, but we had one thing in common: Neither of us really wanted to be a dishwasher. Who did Bob want to be? He wanted to be someone who was loved, respected, valued, and appreciated. Who did *I* want to be? I knew even at sixteen that I wanted to be someone who could make others feel tall, not small, and serve my community as best as I could.

I could have spent that summer wallowing in frustration that I was toiling away in a hot kitchen, scrubbing congealed cheese and curdling soft-serve off piles of dishes and listening to Bob tell me what he thought I should be doing. Bob could have been stuck dealing with a surly teenager whose attitude was bringing everyone down. There were lots of things I could have said that summer that would have made Bob feel tiny and worthless—that I was soon heading off to college, or that I would never spend a summer washing dishes again—but I made the choice to focus not on what I was doing but on the person I was becoming. I let Bob teach me every trick of the trade he knew, and I thanked him for that knowledge at every turn. I listened to him and his dreams. I tried my best to lift him up, because that was the person I aspired to be.

WHO IS THE FOUNDATION FOR *WHAT*

I've had a lot of jobs—from Newport Creamery to the SEALs, the C-suite, and beyond. And while the details of each role—the *what*—absolutely matter, regardless of the level of an organization you're operating at, the *who* matters far more. It's a shame that all too often we start off conversations asking people *what they do* instead of trying to learn about *who they are*, because it's the *who* that will take you to your ultimate destination.

Throughout this book, when I talk about the *who*, I'm really talking about the person you are, deep down, and the life you want to live, a level up from what you actually spend your time doing. Your *who* is formed by the principles that guide you; it's the aspirational person you're hoping to be, the one you see—and want to see—when you look in the mirror. We will grapple with the dissonant details later: the "family man" who spends all day and night at the office; the "powerful business leader" who stepped off the career track to raise kids and doesn't know how to get back on; the "one who has it all" who feels like she's succeeding at none of it; the "underachiever" who's tired of wasting his potential. For now, we're talking vision, and not just in terms of your career. Are you the community builder who brings everyone together? Are you the class clown, ensuring the people around you are always laughing? Are you the "personality hire" who may be half a step slower intellectually but the one individual who can unite the whole office? Are you an adventurer and an explorer? A dreamer? A doer? A caregiver? You may be all of these, or none of them, but you are *someone*, composed of a set of ideas and ideals, interests and passions, goals and guiding lights.

Before I start to take you down the road to figuring out *your who*, it might be helpful for me to share mine. *Who* is Mike Hayes? At my core, I strive to be a person who gives more than he takes, and who gives in a way that unlocks other people's potential. I seek to help everyone understand they are both leaders and followers, and to know when to be which. I aim to grow individuals who can make a difference for even more people, in even more ways. I make efforts to disagree thoughtfully, to help people rise up by considering other viewpoints, and to guide them to land on their own vision without denigrating others for what they believe in. I look to be someone who leverages his own skills in scalable ways to impact others. I work hard to be someone my family and friends can rely upon, turn to in a time of need, and trust with their deepest concerns. I know what good—good work, good performance, good values—looks like, and I try to hold people accountable in constructive ways when they either don't see it or don't do it. I aim to recognize when the people in my life can use me, perhaps even before they know it themselves. I am someone who holds himself and others to the very highest standards. At my best, I am a problem solver, an action taker, and an example of how we as a society can be bringing people together instead of pulling them apart. At the same time, I am someone who is imperfect, who has his own faults and flaws, who comes up short, and is always trying to balance accepting who and where I am with striving to do and be more. Besides "husband," "father," and "brother" on my tombstone, there will be one other word: "patriot," which is why I was driven to serve this country and continue to be driven to do so each and every day.

When you read that paragraph, something may strike you. Not one word in my *who* has anything to do with my job title, my accomplishments, or my bank account. I can be this very same person whether I am a sixty-five-year-old millionaire CEO or a sixteen-year-old kid trying to help his family pay the bills. I can be this person at times of struggle and at times of triumph; when the world is on my side or when everything I do seems like a battle. And I *was* this same person, if I look back thirty years to the beginning of my SEAL career, although I probably wouldn't have used exactly the same words. Back then, I thought a lot about my country and about contributing to something larger than myself. I thought about strength and heroism, impact and achievement. The benchmarks, underneath all of it, were the same. No doubt I am in a different place professionally than I was thirty years ago. And yet, at my core, I am still me.

I bet if you look back at any point in your past, you are much the same now, too.

No matter the stage of your life, I suspect many of the same principles drove you, the same kinds of things made you excited, proud, anxious, or upset as they do today. It's the *what* that changes: your job title, the way you spend your day, the people you surround yourself with, the issues you think about. But the *who* is the person you are, and that person is still you, in every situation and at every point in life.

Sure, success, by any measure, is better than failure. The fact that we start with the *who* doesn't mean that the *what* isn't of critical value, because it is. The *what* is everything: The right *what* fills you up, and the wrong *what* breaks you down. But the *who* comes first. The *who* is conceptual. The *what* is reality. We begin with the *who* because understanding your *who*—deeply, meaningfully, powerfully—is the only way to land on the right *what*, and the gap between your *who* and your *what* is where pretty much all of your disappointments and frustrations lie. The wider the gap, the emptier you feel, and the more you want to run away from your life and start again. Narrow the gap, and you feel whole, satisfied, and yes, Mission Driven. To find the right *what*, you have no choice: You have to start with the *who*.

HOW TO FIND YOUR *WHO*

It's a big question, I know. Who we are and who we want to be are the foundation of everything. They're about the life we want to live, the kinds of people we want to spend time with, the passions that inspire us, the causes we want to fight for, and so much more. When we're children, people ask us, "What do you want to be when you grow up?" but as you're already seeing, that's the wrong question. We should instead be asking our kids, "*Who* do you want to be?" because that will give us far more useful answers.

As she was growing up, I made sure to ask my daughter, Maeson—now a young adult, making her way in the world—*who* she wanted to be (never *what*!), and tried to teach her, along the way, how to get there. We talked, and continue to talk, openly and honestly about principles and values, and about the tools she needs to become that person, and to move closer to her vision.

You probably don't have a crisp *who* just yet. Reading mine might have gotten you thinking, but it would be extraordinary if you were able to fully articulate it on the first try. Then again, the only way to know just how prepared you are is to make a real attempt.

Exercise 1.1

Imagine you step into an elevator and I'm standing there. Let's say it's a tall building and we're going all the way up to the top—so you have some time. I ask you, "Who do you want to be?" You have thirty seconds until we get to our floor. Try it for real, right now. Say it out loud if you can, or in your head if you can't. Thirty seconds. *Who do you want to be?*

I'll wait.

Not easy, is it?

How good was your answer? Did you even come up with a first thought, a first line? Congratulations if so. Many people find themselves tongue-tied, even when doing this exercise by themselves, in their office or on their couch. It is hard to sum ourselves up in a few sentences, especially if we think those sentences have to have meaning—ultimate meaning—and declare our sum total as an individual.

Did you find yourself starting to talk about your career, your family, your hobbies? Everyone has default identities that define them in their own minds. Your answers are not my answers, and your answers shouldn't be the ones you think you're supposed to have if those aren't what resonate for you. Society expects certain things from us, but if those aren't the things you want out of life, then they're not part of your *who* and they're not the elements you should be solving for.

Some people really want to be famous. Some people want to make a lot of money. Or win the Nobel Prize. Those may well be your real goals, and truest motivations, but I do caution against having elements of your *who* that are entirely out of your control. Who you are should be something that you can make happen internally, even on a desert island, outside the constraints of society and without the help of others. I can make myself someone my friends can rely on. I can't make myself famous, and I can't make myself rich, not without some help from the world, help that may or may not come.

In "The Short Game" (chapters 6–10), we'll talk about tactics to try to engineer outcomes like that, but fundamentally, if you find yourself thinking that fame or money is part of your *who*, I would ask you to dig a level deeper. *Why* are those things important to you? If it's because you want to make a difference in some way, use your fame or money to bring about some kind of change, then the fame and the money aren't in fact what you're after. Your *who* is about the change you want to make, not the means to make it. Fame and money can be helpful, no doubt. I can change more lives if I have more money. I can make a greater difference, in some ways, if more people know who I am. But the goal, for me at least, is the impact I can bring to the world, not the fame or the money that might enable it.

You're thinking this is naive, perhaps. You're thinking that all your problems would be solved if you had, say, a billion dollars, or maybe even a couple of orders of magnitude less than that. I will admit that I kind of thought that, too, until I became close friends with a few billionaires. Which I mention only to make the point that everyone has problems, even billionaires, and some of their problems are even bigger simply because they are unconstrained by money. Most billionaires will say they started feeling economically liberated when their net worth reached $10 million, and then at $100 million they felt truly free. But the underlying drive doesn't go away even when you reach $100 million—or the magical billion. The same *who* is still motivating everything they do. Finding a way to be Mission Driven doesn't change just because your bank account grows.

If you unlocked a billion dollars, right now, what would it change about your life? Whatever impact you want to have still requires action of some kind, or at the very least it requires choosing, deciding, weighing options. How much do you give away, on what timeline, and to whom? How do you make that billion dollars do the most good?

And while there are plenty of problems that a billion dollars can solve, it can't make you healthy, happy, or loved, even if you wish it could. Steve Jobs is reported to have said, "My favorite things in life don't cost any money. It's really clear that the most precious resource we all have is time." The point: Everyone is always wrestling with their mission in life. No one has every dimension all figured out.

Look closely at what you articulated in the exercise. Notice your *who* may or may not be about your job. For some, the subject matter of the work they do is really important. "I love music," someone might say, "and so to live my best life, I need to be surrounded by song, helping to bring music to the world, whether as a performer or behind the scenes in some capacity." That's a fine element for a *who*.

Others are moved not as much by the content as by the process. "I want to help talented people—in any sphere—unleash their gifts to the world," and they might be equally fulfilled in a range of roles across many industries. I have moved from finance to the tech world and am currently at a firm at the intersection of both, that finances technology. I'm not a deep technologist or financial expert. The topic, in many ways, matters less to me than the role. I'm a person who loves creating unique value through vision, bringing people together, leading a team, and getting the most out of talented high achievers. Drop me in any setting and that's what I will be driven to do. I don't play an instrument—as I said in *Never Enough*—I conduct bands.

We'll think hard in "The Short Game" about how your *who* can map to the work you might do, but for now it's mostly helpful to realize that the best answers may be a level deeper than your initial response, and it's worth unpacking exactly what moves you, below the surface, and where your gifts and skills actually lie.

To that end, I said in the introduction that this is about *mission*, not *passion*. It's worth reiterating. Some people find themselves believing that their work must also be their passion. To this, my answer is a solid "it depends." What you are passionate to do may or may not line up with what society will pay you for, and that's okay. Some of us are fortunate that the things that move us most are also financially fruitful pursuits, and others need to find ways to construct our lives so that we can achieve the fullest extent of our *who* and at the same time make the kind of economic living we desire. As with everything else, there are no right or wrong answers; there are just answers, and the more you push yourself, the truer those answers will become and the sharper your *who* will be.

Exercise 1.2

Should we try again?

This won't be the last time we do.

Thirty seconds.

Who do you want to be?

Getting clearer?

THE *WHO* MATTERS: AT EVERY STAGE OF LIFE

It is never too early or too late to define your *who*. It's easy at times to put off the hard thinking, especially when wrapped up in the pressure and the adrenaline of the moment-to-moment. I know a lot of SEALs who can't think beyond the SEALs until they find themselves no longer SEALs—and they realize they need something else to fill the rest of their lives. Or said differently, I know very few SEALs who can wrap their head around who they are beyond being a SEAL until they get out. And then the risk of unfulfillment or even depression becomes quite significant, because outside the role, outside the immense responsibility and stakes they've lived with while serving this country, they don't really know *who* they are.

I think about my friend Tim Sheehy, one of my lieutenants in Afghanistan when I was the commander of SEAL Team TWO. Tim was exceptionally brave from the get-go, a fantastic SEAL whose potential for leadership was obvious to everyone around him. I gave him increasing amounts of responsibility, and no matter what I asked him to do, he excelled. I could see that he had a future far beyond the SEAL teams—but I'm not sure if he, just a young man at the time, really knew what he was capable of. He didn't yet fully understand his *who*. My guidance and mentorship to Tim, of course, covered SEAL strategy and tactics, but also the more foundational attributes of life. When Tim left the SEALs, he found new meaning, new purpose. He found exactly *who* he was meant to be. Tim built a remarkable company, and in 2024, he was elected to the US Senate from Montana. What's next for Tim? I don't know, but at thirty-nine years old as I write this, the second-youngest current senator (Jon Ossoff of Georgia is a year younger), he has a lifetime full of choices to make as far as how to achieve his *who*. The only limits to Tim's potential are the ones he decides to put on himself.

I look at my own decisions over time and see that my *who* has become continually clearer. When I left the SEALs, I landed at Bridgewater, the largest hedge fund in the United States and a firm where the kinds of learning and growing I was looking for were absolutely paramount. I'll tell the story of how I got there later on in the book, when discussing how to create the best and right options for yourself, but what I want to focus on here is that when I made the decision to leave the SEALs, I was faced with a bunch of different choices that required me to press hard on my *who* and figure out the person I really wanted to be in the world.

Bridgewater fulfilled much of what I needed, and I loved a lot of elements of the experience, but after three years, I was ready to move on, impatient for something new. Now that I am at an age that starts with a five, I know myself pretty well. Repeatedly in this book, you'll hear me say I'm terrible at patience. It's true, and it's a problem. Impatience can often drive suboptimal decisions. We want change and so we look for the first change we see. Part of the point of being Mission Driven and staying focused on your *who* is about forcing yourself to take the time to be intentional—and not let impatience lead you to make the wrong choices. Once I was ready to leave Bridgewater, it was very hard not to jump at the easiest opportunity that came my way. I could have done that, and fortunately I didn't. You always have to make sure you are running *to* something and not just running *away*. If you're running away, you'll try to convince yourself that any next step is the best one; if you wait until there is something compelling to run toward, you're much more likely to make a better choice.

One of the first opportunities that emerged for me when looking to leave Bridgewater was a substantial one: the chance to run the noninvestment side of the family office of Eric Schmidt, the first CEO of Google and a prominent tech executive and billionaire. The person in that position would be at the very top of the philanthropy world, directing huge amounts of money to address some of the biggest global problems. I went into my interview enthusiastic about the possibilities, and about halfway through the conversation, Eric asked me, "What problem in the world are you most excited to solve?"

I was caught flat-footed. It was, in retrospect, perhaps an obvious question, but it was also such a big one, and I did not have a prepared answer in mind. I had come from environments where the problems we were solving were to a large extent handed to us—SEALs have defined missions; Bridgewater had its own clear business goals. Most people don't have the luxury of working on the problems they most want to solve; instead, we're trying to achieve our own economic freedom, whether that means moving beyond living paycheck to paycheck or trying to build up savings for the future. It's often only after you have security that you can let your ambitions grow.

I wasn't yet at a place where I was thinking as big as Eric was. I imagine he expected a relatively straightforward answer—getting plastics out of the ocean, say, or feeding the hungry in Africa—but for as important as those (and a hundred other things) are in the world, my *who* drove me somewhere else. "The problem I care most about," I said, though less articulately than this, I am sure, "is people participating in the world, and as many of us as possible feeling ownership over our future as a society. Too many people stand on the sidelines when they can and should be making a difference. What drives me isn't the specifics of what someone cares about, but the idea that they care about *something* and that they're acting on it."

"Okay, but how do you solve that?" Eric asked me. "And more specifically for this role, how do you solve it with money?"

I'm good on my feet, but I had to admit I didn't have a strategy for doing that. I hadn't spent any time at all thinking about how to mobilize people to *care*, and I wasn't sure that money was the route to the answer anyway. I realized as I tried to stumble through a response: Figuring out how to spend someone else's money to make a difference in the world might be an interesting challenge, an intellectual exercise at the very least that would have forced me to do a lot of hard thinking, but it also would have taken me away from creating my own direct impact. My *who* was about leading and motivating individuals, not applying money to causes. This wasn't the role for me, and Eric and I both knew it. I'm relieved, looking back, that I didn't try to force the fit and wind up unsatisfied.

That interview did one more thing for me, besides clarifying my *who*: In what may be the ultimate flattery, I stole Eric's interview question—"What problem in the world are you most excited to solve?"—and have asked it of others many times in order to learn about their visions, their plans, and what kind of thinkers they are. I want to know their *who*, or at least understand a piece of it.

I also look back and realize that as I was trying to come up with my answer to Eric's question, I had to try really hard to focus less on what I thought he wanted to hear than on finding my deepest truth. The temptation to think that just because you're sitting in a job interview, that job is the right one to take if you can land it, is very strong. Instead, interviews should be learning opportunities. I'll go much deeper into the interview process in chapter 7, but for now, it's enough to say that it's not necessarily a bad outcome if an interview helps you to better understand that the job isn't the right one for you. I have seen lots of people, ex-SEALs and others, shift their paths along the way as they start to recognize, through life experience, that a road that might have seemed right perhaps isn't. We can—and should—shift and refine goals as we grow. Over time, we learn how we can most meaningfully make the impact we're looking for. You may think, for instance, that you want to make change through the political system. But after pursuing it for a while, you might realize the change you want to make is in another sphere entirely. Ultimately the only way you gain knowledge about yourself is by doing *something* in the first place. Over time, you iterate to get closer and closer to what's right for your *who*.

The sooner in life you start operating under this approach, the more time you have to experiment and eventually land on the best and most rewarding opportunities. Investments of all kinds—including investments in yourself and your ability to engineer impact—grow over years. It's the magic of compounding, and it applies to everything. There are people who worry that they can't apply a Mission Driven mindset until they have financial security, or until they settle down to raise a family—or even until they retire—but if all you do is put up obstacles, you are setting yourself up for a lifetime of disappointment. No matter the milestone you set as the time to finally make a difference, when you get there, the goal-posts will be all too easy to move. When I was a twenty-two-year-old SEAL, the thought of having $50 in my wallet felt like financial freedom. With age, with a family, with responsibilities, that number obviously changed. And if I had told myself I couldn't try to make a difference until I was feeling completely secure with my own economic situation, it would have never happened. I'd be putting aside my own mission until it was far too late, and the gap between my *who* and my *what* would be forever growing.

The best way to set yourself up for a Mission Driven life—start to finish—is by engaging in the process of building your future as early as possible. Make the kinds of investments in your *who* right now that will pay off for the rest of your years. I often tell people to focus on the foundation; the walls and the roof can come later. Think about the net present value of investing now to get closer to your *who*, of making sacrifices that will bear fruit in the future. This means taking meetings and building relationships even if they may not pay off for decades to come. It means pushing to do the hard things. It means education, focus, and creating options. You don't see the curve of life until you've already lived it. Early experiences often pay off in surprising ways.

And yet at the same time as I say it's never too soon, it's also never too late. I talk to people contemplating retirement but who aren't sure what they'll do with their time and energy once their professional purpose is gone. The answer again comes right back to the *who*. Elevated job titles may be a thing of the past for someone in this position, but if you have distilled what brings you meaning and purpose, then the title doesn't matter. There are always ways to fulfill a mission outside the professional sphere, without the trappings of power and influence you might have gotten used to. My friend Frank D'Souza, the cofounder and former CEO and vice chairman of Cognizant, a technology and consulting firm with over 350,000 employees and now $20 billion in annual revenue, had more success at a young age than most people will have in a lifetime. I worked with Frank as Cognizant's senior vice president and head of strategic operations after leaving Bridgewater, and he is like a brother to me. One of the things I admire most about Frank is that he sees his success not as an end in itself but as a means to lift others up and enable *their* success. Now in his next phase of positively impacting the world, Frank fulfills his mission as the founder of a private equity firm, Recognize, with over $2 billion in regulatory assets under management, still creating enormous value, but doing it to be even more impactful in the ways that matter to him and his family.

Frank understands that what matters most isn't how much is coming in but how much is going out, and what money is being used for. Executing on the principle of creating value for others makes it easy for him to make decisions.

For people who picked up this book thinking about a post-work life, this may well be the first time you have the bandwidth to explore the facets of your *who* you have yet to achieve. That brings with it freedom and possibility, but also pressure and obligation. In late 2023, I had three months—the first time in my adult life I've ever had a real break—between ending my role as chief operating officer at VMware, the cloud computing giant we sold to Broadcom for $69 billion, and starting my next opportunity at Insight Partners, the private equity firm where I moved next, helping to select and grow our portfolio of 600 technology companies, creating value for our investors, the portfolio companies, and their buyers. On one level, in three months there are almost no wrong choices, and if my wife and I had decided to take a trip around the world, I don't think there would have been anything wrong with that. But you can always look to your *who* to figure out what might instead give you a greater reward.

I thought about the kinds of things I hadn't ever had time to do but were still really important to me—the elements of my *who* that perhaps I neglected when I was under pressure professionally and didn't have a lot of bandwidth to spare. Part of the person I strive to be is someone with family at the center of his life, but there have absolutely been times when, intentionally or inadvertently, I have made other choices. I mean, for a large part of my career, I was deployed overseas for stretches of six months or more—I had seven deployments of that length, taking me away from my wife and daughter—and while I don't regret any of it, I know there was plenty I missed, and that it was a sacrifice on all sides.

Faced with three months of downtime, I made a choice to finally go through sixty-two hours of video footage (and countless photos) that my grandparents had taken of themselves and our family—video footage I had never had the chance to watch—and digitize it, catalog it, and store it in a way that generations to come can watch to see what the ancestors they never had a chance to meet were actually like. It was a privilege to do this for my extended family, bringing me great reward, and fulfilling a piece of my overall mission that was often getting sidelined by more pressing concerns.

Along similar lines, I spent much of those three months working on this book, because I knew that my time would be more pressured once my new job started, and I desperately wanted to be sure that I got these ideas down on paper. Helping others become Mission Driven is such a core part of the legacy I want to create in and for the world—but it's also hard to write a book when you're working a full-time-plus job.

The reality of every life is that pressures are different at different times, and our decisions about how to spend our time change depending on responsibilities—more on that in "The Short Game." Having a crisp *who* gives you a touchstone to refer back to whenever you're not quite sure how to find the greatest meaning.

A *WHO* WITH IMPACT: BUT WHAT KIND?

Before we dive a level deeper into crafting our own *who*, I want to call out *impact* a little more specifically. I talk a lot about impact. We all want to have impact. But impact can mean a lot of different things, and it's easy to skip the hard thinking about exactly what kind of impact we want to have. I talk to so many SEALs who say they love the job because of the impact they know they're making. "I love being part of the mission; I love making a difference," they might say, and 100 out of 100 SEALs would agree with that—but there are two questions that should naturally follow. First, is this mission the highest and best use of your time (an opportunity cost question)? Second, and maybe even more dramatically, is your mission making the world *better*? What if a particular mission makes the world *worse*? If all you're thinking about is making a difference—without thinking about the kind of difference you're making—then you run the risk of wasting resources you could be deploying for far greater value.

Obviously no SEAL mission is ever designed to make the world worse, or less safe, but there are lots of ways people spend their energy that may, in fact, be harmful rather than helpful, or at least harmful depending on someone's perspective. This is not a political point, and this is not a political book, but I pose this idea to make sure you're thinking about the content of your impact and not just the impact itself. I don't want to ever find myself on a mission that increases polarization, for instance, or pulls people away from one another. I don't want to help us all spend more time on screens and less time with our fellow citizens, or to help turn up the volume on misinformation and confuse people about the reality around them. These are easy things to say, but there is always a danger we find ourselves so deep in a particular foxhole that we miss the bigger picture. Lots of people see trees, but to have success, you also need to see the forest.

If you pushed most SEALs to think deeper, they would talk about freedom and democracy and wanting to make sure that people around the world have the same kind of privilege as we do in America to live our lives without fear and with hope for future generations. And I trust that if we each think about the substance of the impact we want to make, we will land on something great. But it's not automatic. When I went on SEAL missions, no matter the details of the assignment itself, I needed to think bigger: I wasn't just looking to stop extremists like the Taliban or ISIS; even more rewarding was to be able to keep people from becoming violent extremists in the first place. I wanted to figure out why the pipeline building terrorists was effective and change the incentives so that the world would have fewer dangerous people in it. I wanted to find ways to incentivize more people to positively influence others with their own capacity. I describe a SEAL's job simply: stop bad people from doing bad things to good people. But the higher calling is to stop bad people from becoming bad in the first place, and to turn those who have become bad back into good people instead.

None of this is to say that your impact needs to be big enough to change the world. It doesn't. Changing the world is really just lots of little impacts in the right direction all added together. I look at one of my aunts, a Catholic nun who devoted her life to helping just a handful of people in the most profound ways, and I can't say that she had less impact than serving in the White House and moving the dial on some large issue for a giant population by an infinitesimal amount. You can push super-deep on one thing for your whole life and help a few people quite meaningfully, or you can touch many, just a drop, and either way is fantastic, as long as you do it with intention. You will spend a few hours with this book, hopefully it will help you a bit, and then you'll move on. It won't necessarily change your life in noticeable ways, but if it pushes you just a little, then it's been worth it—worth your time to read, and my time to write. I trust that's enough. Every little bit counts, as long as it pushes you closer to achieving your *who*.

Exercise 1.3

SO *WHO* ARE YOU?

We're going to do it now, together. Take out a 3-by-5 index card—because your *who* probably shouldn't be bigger than that, or if it is, you're including too much.

I feel so strongly that you need to put these words on paper that I've left space below. Make copies, even—or write in pencil. You don't have to get this right the first time. You've tried the elevator pitch already, but now you've had a few more pages to think, and to reflect on what truly matters to you.

It can be instructive to think of the *who* as a vision statement for a person, no different from a vision statement for a company. There are plenty of companies with visions that we, even as mere consumers, can articulate pretty easily. Airbnb, according to its mission statement, wants to create a world where anyone can belong any-where. Google wants to organize the world's information in a uni-versally accessible and useful way. Bridgewater wants to understand the world and then predict the macroeconomic flows of resources.

Those are all compelling, and even as we might debate the details of whether each company always lives up to its goal—just as we will not always live up to our own aspirational *who*—the intent is quite clear. Of course, those three firms will be gone eventually—in 30 years, 100 years, 500 years, we don't know—just like we'll be gone, too—but the hope is that they and we will have made the world bet-ter in some small or large way.

So what is that way? What is *your* legacy? What is your intent with your life? Here's some space to try, if you don't have an index card:

_____

_____

_____

_____

_____

_____

Before you declare yourself finished, I'd urge you to think about other people in your life and what you think their *who* state-ments would or should be. As you refine your *who*, reflect on how you see others around you, how you think they see themselves, and how you think they see you. We often recognize things in others that they don't realize they're putting out into the world. The peo-ple close to us, in fact, sometimes know us even better than we know ourselves.

I met Virginia Governor Glenn Youngkin over a decade ago, years before he had ever thought about going into public service. We had breakfast, just the two of us. He felt like a friend I'd known forever, and I could see instantly, crystal-clearly that he was a great human being. I could see what motivated him and what gave him energy. I told him I saw his future in public service. He was a leader in the private equity world at the time, making a difference and creating value by bringing meaningful companies public, taking them private, merging them, or helping them in a myriad of other ways. He saw that as his life's work. After talking to him, I was certain that he would be a future national leader serving the public in a very different way. He hadn't yet figured it out, but as he later did, his trajectory was and is limitless. Regardless of your personal politics (and I say this as someone who served Presidents George W. Bush and Barack Obama and have enormous respect for them both, as I have for many, many individuals from both major political parties, and individuals from neither party. It is about the person, not the party; the ideas, not the ideology; the truth, not the distorted picture we get of so many of the good people committed to serving us, in all ways, and from all directions), I share the story to make the point: others know, others see.

Sadly, sometimes you learn the most about someone's *who* at their funeral. I was at Arlington National Cemetery for the funeral of my friend Dr. Shannon Kula Clark—an inspiring patriot, Capitol Hill staffer, and aspiring congresswoman—who died of breast cancer in the summer of 2023 at the age of forty-eight, much too early, much too soon. Shannon was the chief of staff for Senator Barbara Mikulski and worked on everything from women's health issues to national security appropriations. As the wife of my dear friend, White House Fellow and retired Marine Lieutenant Colonel Ron Clark, former Deputy Under Secretary of the Department of Homeland Security, and former acting Senior Director of the Defense Directorate in the National Security Council, Shannon understood military issues and worked so hard to fight for our service members, spouses, and veterans. There was a string of testimonials read at her graveside, first from relatives and friends, then from senators and governors...and finally from President Joe Biden, calling Shannon a friend of his, and talking about how she moved the nation. What could be more impactful than a president earnestly calling you a friend—while at the same time having the people closest to you also feel deeply moved and affected by your life?

I know Shannon recognized the good she had created in the world, but I don't know if she fully recognized the magnitude of her impact and inspiration on and for so many.

Which is why I urge you to give the people around you a chance to react to your *who*, and for you to respond to theirs, before it's too late. Know the difference that others feel like you've made and express the difference you have felt from the actions of others. I've been to way too many SEAL funerals to ever feel confident I'll have another chance to tell someone how much I respect and honor them.

Speaking of SEAL funerals, the common theme at all of them is that these were people who died doing what they loved, with and for people they loved as well. I know this may come out sounding a bit dark, but as you formulate your *who*, don't hold back. Think big: Aspire to do something worth dying for. Better yet, *be someone* worth dying for.

What do you want people to say at your funeral?

DO YOU HAVE THE RIGHT *WHO*?

You've now had three chances in this book—two elevator pitches and the space I gave you a couple of pages ago—to craft your own *who*. I've been purposely a bit vague about the specific elements you might want to consider, not wanting to bias you in one direction or another. I don't want to provide examples, aside from my own near the start of the chapter just to lay the groundwork for the discussion. Instead, I've wanted to leave things open so that you can land on what is most meaningful to you, without being pushed to come up with a carbon copy of someone else's *who*. After all, we are each unique. Even if we were to strive to be the "perfect" person, that perfect person would look different in each of our minds.

And we don't just want to write down our version of the perfect person, to be clear; we want to write down the honest version of ourselves, and who we are even if it's not who we sometimes wish we were. If you know you're never going to be motivated to go to the gym, no matter how much you think you should be, then a *who* that pretends you're a person who is going to lift a bunch of weights is only going to lead to a mismatch when you try to map it to the details of the life you are actually living.

That said, it's important to remember that your *who* should be aspirational. We don't always live up to it, but it's a statement of who we are aiming to be, not an admission of the flaws we've come to accept within ourselves. Your *who* also doesn't have to be exhaustive and include all the things you care about. In fact, it shouldn't. You should edit it down to what really gets you excited to wake up in the morning. Anything more than that is filler.

If you get to the right 3-by-5 card, this becomes your touchstone for every decision you make. Ask: Is what you are doing contributing to your *who*, or not making all that much of a difference? If it's not contributing, maybe you're on the wrong track.

For people who are really having trouble, I do want to end this chapter with a bit of guidance, because I want you to move on to chapter 2 with a crisp, clear articulation of your *who*—not that it can't and won't change. As you continue thinking, you might want to ask yourself a few questions:

- Would you rather have deep impact on a smaller scale, or perhaps more limited impact on a larger scale?
- Do you lean into intervening in the problems of others or wait for them to come to you?
- Are there big-picture issues that move you—innovation, education, the environment, etc.?
- How do you decide what is worth doing?
- How is your focus split between your family, your community, and the world?
- How calm are you when things get hard? Do you thrive when you're pushed or when you're comfortable?
- Are your answers the same if you are the only one who will see them?

I could write a hundred more questions, and as we proceed in this book, many more questions will emerge in the chapters to come—but this is a start. We'll come back to your *who* again and again throughout the book, and you may well use a dozen more 3-by-5 cards as you keep refining. We don't need to lock in on our *who* just yet, but take what you have into the next chapter, where we start to map the *who* to the realities of the world and figure out what, for you, personally and professionally, might end up defining robust and undeniable success.

CHAPTER TWO

Defining Success

My wife, Anita (goes by "Ni"), did not appear much on the page in my first book, but I think her story is a perfect example of how success doesn't have to mean the same thing for everyone. The truth is there is another version of history where she's the writer of this book, not me, and it's overflowing with the kind of wisdom, warmth, and humor that has kept me going through our nearly thirty years together. My own success is driven in so many ways by Ni knowing exactly what I needed at any given moment: to be helped and supported, picked up off the floor, or brought down a notch in a moment of hubris. Ni is an amazing human being, a talented artist, an inspiring mentor, and a devoted wife and mother—and her success in all of those endeavors stems from the reality that purpose and meaning can flow into our lives from all different directions.

I make the case to people a generation younger than I am, just starting their careers, that it's so hard to be a "successful" full-time parent and a "successful" full-time professional at once. In fact, I don't believe anyone can do it, at least not without a lot of help. If we're skilled, we can achieve about one and a half of those two ambitions—an all-in worker and a part-time parent, or a full-time parent with some inevitable limitations on our career—and if we're lucky, the people around us pick up the rest. My career in particular, especially when our daughter, Maeson, was young, was not the kind that allowed me to be present in the way I wish I could have been. I understood the trade-off, of course, but that didn't make it any less difficult. When I was home, Maeson had my attention, for sure—but when I was commanding SEALs halfway across the world, my bandwidth for anything else was limited. I tried to make up for a lack of quantity time with quality time, but kids need both. It diminishes Ni's formidable accomplishments to say she was a full-time parent while I was deployed abroad—indeed, when I think about the work she has done over the years (earning a master's degree from the Harvard Extension School; leading architects and builders on several massive home improvement projects, drawing sketches and creating innovative, functional designs; amassing an impressive portfolio of artwork; years of daily hands-on care for relatives facing extreme health challenges, and so on, and so on), it sometimes amazes me how much she was able to accomplish while I was away. But we decided together that her ability to be flexible for Maeson was important, and it gave me great comfort knowing that Ni was making up for my periods of absence from our daughter's day-to-day life.

All military families with young children deal with these choices—of course, all families with young children where at least one parent has a job that takes them away for more hours than their kids are in school have to figure out how to make things work. If they're in a position where the economics don't force their hand, they have to choose what to sacrifice and whether the rewards of full-time work (and I can acknowledge there are plenty: money, passion, socialization, having an independent element of your life) exceed the price of not being able to be always present and at the bus stop at the end of the day, hugging your child, offering her a snack, and listening to her tell you about her day. The landscape has changed since the Covid pandemic, with more people able to work from home and quite possibly be more physically present—but someone's emotional presence is oftentimes a different story. I sit here writing these pages with a twenty-four-year-old daughter, not a kindergartener, but I am not convinced I know the answer as to whether it's better to have a parent who's physically there 100% of the time but constantly on their computer or on their phone, trying to impossibly juggle work and family at once, or a parent who's gone six months out of the year but completely focused when they're present.

Our decision to have Ni prioritize parenting was the right one for our family, and it wasn't just about our daughter. Service isn't something that only the service member performs. Knowing that Ni was managing our day-to-day life at home freed me not to worry about it and get distracted from the mission overseas. Reality is reality, and I saw some of my fellow SEALs stressed all the time, not about what we were doing in Iraq or Afghanistan, but because they just talked to their wife and found out their bathroom had flooded, or their one car broke down and their kids had no way of getting to a dental appointment. Spouses play a pivotal role in helping a SEAL Team be more mission ready, because knowing things are being handled at home is a giant relief and very genuinely contributes to mission success overseas.

I am not trying to make the case that one parent in every family ought to be at home. I saw situations that worked and situations that didn't, in all permutations. What I saw most of all was spouses feeling needlessly embarrassed when asked, "What do you do?" If they were 1.0 parent and 0.5 professional, they didn't want to talk about their work, and if they were 1.0 professional and 0.5 parent, they didn't want to deal with other people's judgment about who was raising their kids. We all need to recognize that these are hard choices and the right answer is the answer that works for you and your family, maps to your *who*, and makes you feel as good as you can when you wake up in the morning. And we need to understand that judging others should never be an element of anyone's *who*.

My definition of success when I was in the SEALs was easy: Was my team succeeding in our missions? If you can't find a compelling mission as a SEAL, you're simply in the wrong line of work, because impact is obvious and can't be denied. Ni's definition of success was a lot harder. She had to think about the best ways to create impact at home and carve a life for herself within the uncertainty of my fate overseas and the challenges of effectively being a single parent. For many years, her success was in part about helping other families navigate these challenges, and alongside everything else she was doing, she mentored many younger SEAL spouses who sought guidance about military life. Some of that guidance was practical—here is what you do when your car hasn't yet arrived from your previous duty station and your husband is already overseas, or here's the doctor who'll give your kid a quick physical so you can get the forms signed mid-year and he can start school—but a lot of it was emotional, and much like the advice in this book: how spouses could find their own place in the world, and live a Mission Driven life even though they were the ones back at home.

It is really important, as you start to test your *who*, to recognize that success can be big and success can be small. You can spread democracy around the world or you can make sure your child has a healthy meal on the table. What matters isn't what anyone else thinks. Defining success is intensely personal, even when society seems to push us in particular directions. I've never met anyone who didn't feel the pressure of living up to everyone else's definition of success, but if you can catch yourself—whether you worry that you're being judged or you feel yourself starting to judge someone else—and reframe the question, then you're way ahead of most people. It's not about "Am I successful in someone else's eyes?" but about "How am I defining success?"

DEFINING SUCCESS: TURNING DOWN THE NBA

I spent time in the summer of 2024, while working on this book, trying to help a friend answer exactly this question: *How should I define success?* Dan Hurley, the legendary University of Connecticut basketball coach, reached out after he read *Never Enough*. I came and spoke to his team—and saw his inspiring approach. They ended up winning the national championship. I came back the next year. They won again. Along the way, Dan and I became great friends, calling on each other for advice and support. And then, Dan received an offer to coach the Los Angeles Lakers—for more money than he could have ever imagined, a reported six-year $70 million contract. Winning those back-to-back championships at UConn, with a 68–11 record over those two seasons and numerous College Coach of the Year awards, made him a hot commodity. After fourteen seasons as a college coach (six years at UConn following stints at the University of Rhode Island and Wagner College in New York), many coaches would have seen the jump to the NBA as a no-brainer, even without considering the money. After all, the NBA would be seen by most as the pinnacle of the profession. But not everyone's definition of success is the same.

When Dan wanted to talk, I knew he didn't need to know what *I* would do in his shoes; what I would do didn't matter. Instead, he needed to clarify and pressure-test what mattered to *him*, and then he needed to figure out what option was going to get him to his *who*, on his own terms. The biggest driver that Dan initially expressed was his ability to make such a positive impact in the lives of the highly talented young men who played for him. Of course, another consideration was a desire to try for a three-peat at UConn. Only one team in NCAA history has ever won more than two titles in a row. Back in the late 1960s and early 1970s, the UCLA Bruins were dominant, winning nine out of ten championships between 1964 and 1973, including the last seven in a row, starting in 1967. It was a different game back then, and the chance to accomplish a similar feat with UConn couldn't be ignored.

But remember what I said about situations that are out of your control. Dan and his players could certainly work toward the goal of winning three in a row, but there had to be more than that. Victory in sports is always going to involve some amount of luck and good fortune, so I wondered: Were there ways that Dan could define success that didn't hinge entirely on the outcome of a series of basketball games?

On one level, were there attributes of a successful team that were the real measures of success? Were the teams that were most likely to win the most agile, the most prepared, the most inspired? If the team was going to lose—no matter what—was there a way for Dan to feel, at the end of the season, like he had been successful anyway, or was it a failure if he didn't capture a third consecutive trophy? I didn't want to answer these questions for him, but I wanted to help him think in those terms, to separate the pieces he was going to be able to control from the results that would be out of his hands.

On another level, aside from team success, what did Dan want? What did success mean to him, putting the three-peat aside? In chapter 7, we'll go through the vectors that everyone making a career choice should be thinking about: the importance of geography, prestige, money, and a dozen other factors that you need to explore, consider, and rank. But on top of it all is mission. While the job of NBA coach and the job of college basketball coach are the same in some ways, they are different in a few respects, chief among them the players and where they are in life. As a college coach, Dan explained to me, you are influencing young adults—kids, really—who are still looking for their place in the world, still figuring out their own journeys, and you get a chance as a coach to shape, mentor, and impact their lives. In the NBA, you're important, but in a different way. You're managing adults—wealthy, successful, famous adults—and helping them navigate that life. It's not insignificant, but it's also not the same. The kind of player management and development that a coach is doing in the NBA is different from what goes into the role at the college level. There are going to be people who gravitate toward one or the other, who feel like they can make a bigger difference in one of those roles. Which role did Dan want to play? I didn't have answers; I just had the questions.

Dan was in a fortunate position where there probably wasn't a wrong choice to make—he was going to make millions of dollars regardless and be at the helm of an elite basketball program, with an opportunity to perform at the highest level and make a real impact on players, fans, and families. The goal for all of us should be to get into positions like his, even if on a much smaller scale, where we have choices, multiple entities valuing what we can do for them and offering us enviable opportunities. But that's not the end of the process; it's only the beginning. It is easy to let the expectations of others drive our definitions of success, and it's far too easy to be seduced by someone else's vision. No one would have blamed Dan for saying yes to the Lakers. In fact, most people would have expected it. But when he reflected on what he really wanted at this point in his life, tuning out the noise and focusing on what mattered to him, the answer emerged. He signed a six-year, $50 million contract—leaving tens of millions of dollars on the table—to stay with UConn.

WHAT IS SUCCESS FOR YOU?

Dan's story is hard to relate to in some ways. He was going to be a multimillionaire regardless. Both of his choices were great ones. But the point stands: It's still a choice, and in Dan's shoes, it was a real one, with high stakes and lots of emotion. You have your 3-by-5 card, or the *who* you drafted on the page in chapter 1, but mapping it to the real world can be difficult. Dan Hurley didn't write his *who* on the page, but I heard it in our conversations: He wanted to be someone who made a real impact in his players' lives, and build the kinds of relationships it's much harder to build with millionaires in the NBA. Without that element of the job, he was not going to feel like a true success.

So let's jump to you, and start where you are right now. Look at your life and ask yourself: What's working and what's missing? Do you consider yourself, right at this moment, a successful person? The fact that you picked up this book probably means on some level you know there's more you can do. You're trying to figure out what's out there and how you can achieve it. One of the best ways to figure out what you're missing from your life is to study the people around you whom you admire. This can be tricky, because we only see the parts of people's lives they make visible to us, and we make assumptions that aren't always correct.

One of the executives who worked hard to convince me to come to Bridgewater had a nine-figure balance sheet from a company he had founded and sold. By any external measure, he was a standout success. A married father of six with multiple luxury homes, he jumped out of a twentieth-story hotel window and killed himself. He wrote in his suicide note that the pain of messing up—he used a different word—was just too great. I hadn't talked to him in a few years, but I liked him a lot, and from my perspective, he was a high-energy, very successful person. I don't know what was going on in his life, and I desperately wish he would have gotten the help he needed, but he is just one of countless examples of people whose inside voices don't sound like we might expect them to from the external markers we see.

It doesn't have to be so dramatic. You may think that your neighbor is successful because she has a good job title, a family that seems happy, and a new car in the driveway. But do you know what she's measuring herself against and what she's trying to achieve? You can't ever know someone else's *who*, at least not until you ask them. And that's the next exercise.

Exercise 2.1

After you feel good about the *who* you've put down on paper, I want you to question a few of the people in your life about their own definitions of success and how they feel about their lives. This is the first step in our crowdsourcing, asking others to reflect on themselves—before we ask them to reflect on us a bit later in the chapter. These are conversations we're not used to having, and the mere act of asking someone to engage in a conversation like this can have the valuable side benefit of bringing that person closer to you.

Pick five people in your life who you believe have reached some level of success, however you want to define it, and then reach out to ask for twenty minutes—which will sometimes stretch longer if you do it right—to talk about success. Frame it as a fact-finding mission: Tell them you're engaged in your own exploration of success and clarifying your mission in life. Tell them you admire them and would love their help in figuring out what success can mean to different people. Ask them if they consider themselves successful and see what they say. Ask how they measure their success and see how much their answers do or don't resonate for you.

Perhaps everyone you pick will tell you things you already suspect about how they view their lives—but it's more likely there will be a few surprises. It is also the case that not everyone is realistic about the world, and their place in it, or will be honest with you about their worries and doubts. Not everyone is willing or able to be vulnerable. You may catch someone at a moment when they are more open, or less open. Not everyone is truthful with themselves, and some people may not be able to admit where they struggle or have struggled in the past. But hearing how others view their success can give you insight into how to look at your own life and perhaps new perspectives on how to approach the question for yourself.

Have an open mind, but be cautious to not be overly influenced by other people's definitions of success. Theirs should not be automatically adopted as your own. We risk being thrown off our true paths by family or friends or societal expectations. So many people struggle with understanding what success means *for them*. It is one of the most important questions of our life, because if we don't know what we are aiming for, we can't ever get there.

There is a bias some of us have to think that the "right" definition of success is to be selfless like Mother Teresa. But that is neither realistic nor desirable for most people—and that's okay! Part of the goal of this chapter is to help you understand that success comes in all forms, and the point is to be intentional about the path you are on, and to use this book as a springboard to get yourself headed in the best and right direction.

CONSUMPTION, AMBITION, AND OTHER NEEDLESS SOURCES OF SHAME

I am as human as anyone else. I bought an expensive watch as my one splurge after Broadcom bought VMware. And I admit I'm still sometimes conflicted about it. I try to keep it tucked up my sleeve out of sight, and on the occasions I've seen people notice it on my wrist, I feel self-conscious. It's red, white, and blue, and every time I look at it, it reminds me of America, what we stand for as a nation, the people I've been privileged to serve alongside, and my lifelong mission to my SEAL brothers who are no longer here. I share this to say that it's okay to want material things, and to include that as part of your definition of success—as long as you understand what those material goods can and can't bring to your life. They won't make you happy, at least not that I've experienced, but certain things can, of course, make your life easier and more comfortable.

I want to be honest and transparent throughout this book, and part of that is acknowledging the very real pull that money can have on us. It's okay to want to be able to afford a mortgage on a house in a nice neighborhood. It's okay to want to be able to give your children the things they desire. It's okay to want to eat in fancy restaurants and go on nice vacations. Wanting these things and also wanting to make an impact and help the people around you do not have to be contradictory goals. Sometimes people fall into a trap of thinking money shouldn't factor into their decisions—or that a "good" person wouldn't make decisions based on money—but that's an anti-constructive way to look at it. Making money—if that's something that drives you—is useful because it means you can do more to effect the kind of change you want to see in the world, whether that involves giving the money away or using the money to build the kinds of companies or organizations that can produce great value. Money creates flexibility for the present—allowing you to buy yourself time in order to execute your mission (paying others to clean your house, make your food, etc.). It also creates optionality for the future, in case you later want to do something more focused on service, with fewer economic rewards.

People sometimes think the career paths that lead to certain levels of wealth require sacrifices to one's ideals. Careers in finance and related fields are weighed down by many assumptions, both positive and negative—but the more people you meet who pursue these paths, the more you realize they are motivated by the same mix of things we all are and shouldn't necessarily be painted with the broad brush of stereotypes. And sometimes pursuing one of those careers for a limited amount of time can allow someone to then do other things they may also be suited for, opening up paths that might have otherwise been impossible.

Money is a means to an end, nothing more and nothing less. It can help you achieve your *who*, whether that *who* involves providing for yourself and your family or something more. Money allows you to be more purposeful about your choices over the course of your life, buying freedom as you age. All along the way, we make decisions about whether to raise our quality of life today or save for tomorrow. In our youth, we can build our foundation as much as we can, and then later on we can maximize the variables most important to us.

I felt some amount of judgment when I left the SEALs and went to Bridgewater—and maybe it was all in my head, but I worried that people would think I was making a selfish choice that changed my highest priority from making a difference in the world to chasing money instead. One truth is that in moving to Bridgewater, I felt confident I was choosing the hardest thing I could do and maximizing my own learning in service of expanding opportunities down the line. Another truth is that making money can become a powerful vehicle for doing extraordinary good for the world—paying off Gold Star widows' mortgages make up twelve of the most emotional and favorite days of my life. The people who ultimately make the greatest difference in our world are the ones who do make money and then turn around and use that money to engineer tremendous change, Bill Gates, Warren Buffett, and Mackenzie Bezos among them.

In short, you can still be a good person if you spend a week on the beach somewhere warm instead of building houses for the homeless. Build those houses if you can, absolutely—but it doesn't diminish your impact if you choose to help in other ways instead. There is a difference between intellectually wanting to live a certain way and feeling it in your gut. In that spirit, I've already talked about the dangers of external definitions of success, but I want to acknowledge that for some people the reality is that external approval can be important. Certainly, it can lead to the ability to make a greater impact. But for some people, too, the external approval simply makes them feel better. We can have multiple motives for desiring certain things. Some people want a lofty job title because it means more money, others want the influence the lofty title will bring, and others just feel good about themselves because they have the title. There's no judgment here for which of those motivations drives you, just the insistence that you don't act blindly. Be honest with yourself about what you need to feel successful and then be deliberate about the choices you make in pursuit of your goals.

Along the same lines, there is nothing wrong with trying to be famous if you are going to use that fame in a positive way. While "likes" are not, in my opinion, the most productive thing to spend your time chasing, that kind of external approval really does make some people feel better. Fame can also bring opportunities to increase your reach as an individual. The fame of someone like Taylor Swift or Kim Kardashian creates a platform that allows them to move millions of people. But to make a difference, they have to use that platform with intention.

Elite athletes struggle as well with these types of issues. Detroit Lions tight end Sam LaPorta was on Coach Kirk Ferentz's University of Iowa college football team when I gave a talk about what it means to be a team and a teammate. After Sam was the thirty-fourth overall pick in the 2023 NFL Draft, he and I had a great conversation about impact on the nation and the world and how in some ways that transcends on-the-field success. His success and the team's success would, of course, be defined by on-field records and statistics, but he wanted to also keep his own broader success in mind.

I pushed Sam on the same things you are finding in these pages: *Who* do you want to be and how can you use your platform to be a positive force for this great nation? We also talked about how it's okay if he didn't have it all figured out before he even reported to his first training camp. Knowing you want to have that larger impact is the critical first step. And in all cases, putting your energy into your primary job and being the best you can be is what creates the strongest platform from which you can produce those great outcomes.

There is no one with a bigger heart and head than Sam. He's an exceptional person who I'm certain will be a great leader—on and off the field—for many years to come. And in his rookie year, he set NFL records for most receptions, receiving yards, and touchdowns by a rookie tight end. He was also one of the few rookies selected to play in the Pro Bowl. Great things happen to great people. And great people make great things happen.

Hand in hand with thinking about the issues of money and fame is the somewhat more nebulous concept of ambition. Ambition is very much the concrete application of our *who*: It means having a goal we're working toward and a level of determination around attaining it. The intensity around that desire is ambition, which makes ambition a great thing when it's taking us to the right place, and potentially a harmful quality when it leads us astray. This is again why defining success correctly is so critical. Ambition is the fuel that drives the train faster and faster, so we want to be sure it's headed to the right station.

High-performing individuals fall into a dangerous trap when they act without having a crystal-clear destination in mind; their ambition can move them quickly, but who knows where they'll end up? It can become far too easy to work toward another's definition of success instead of our own. But that won't feel like true success in the end. "I did all the work and made partner at my law firm," someone might say, but then eventually find it's not satisfying and not enough. That's because ambition might have moved them forward without a careful consideration of what success as a firm lawyer would mean. For some people, that success is exactly what they're looking for, but for others it may not be.

One of the masters of ambition I had the privilege to work with was Pat Gelsinger, the former CEO of VMware and Intel. When he was at VMware, where I served as chief digital transformation officer (before later becoming chief operating officer), Pat held people to an ambitiously high standard and pushed them to accomplish even more than they ever imagined. When there was a big conference coming up, he would start with the announcement of what his team was going to achieve and the date it needed to be achieved by—and let his team figure out how to get there. Many people would say that his pushes were impossible, and sometimes they were. But sometimes they weren't—and extraordinary breakthroughs were achieved. Pat was always pushing, because he knew that if he didn't push, no one would. When he left VMware, in my last meeting with him, Pat urged me to continue to set and uphold high standards. "Without that pressure, VMware's performance will be mediocre." He was right. Ambition can help provide the pressure we need to succeed.

You can agree with me about all of this, or you don't have to. You can decide that money is evil and ambition is worse. That's okay. I get it. What this chapter is all about is recognizing that the only arguments that matter are the ones that you yourself believe in. You get to define your own version of success, whether that means making money, making peace, or making a wonderful home for your family. The worst things you can do are let others define what your life ought to look like and feel ashamed about what it is that drives you.

PRESSURE TESTING YOUR SUCCESS DEFINITION

There's a simple question you can ask in order to figure out if your definition of success is the right one: If you achieve it, will it bring you closer to your *who*?

There is no one-size-fits-all path. There are people who thrive when every moment of their day is scheduled and purposeful, and others who need downtime and inward focus to make their most profound impact. Where you fall on that spectrum is personal, and what moves you is up to you alone. If the markers you're judging yourself by don't feel right, the task isn't to work harder to reach them, but rather to adjust them.

Pressure testing whether you're aiming for the right kind of success is really hard. It's very difficult to be objective and reflective about yourself, even in cases where you are able to judge others. In the SEALs, we tried to tease out objectivity through a feedback process you can apply to your own life. I know your life is not a SEAL mission, but we can still debrief just as rigorously.

In the corporate world, companies often engage in 360-degree feedback sessions for employees to better understand how they are doing. This is something no one thinks to bring to their personal lives, but there is no reason we can't, and in fact, it can be much more powerful when applied not just to the workplace but to our entire holistic self. The term *360-degree feedback* refers to engaging all the people who work with you—managers, peers, and everyone around you in an organization—to help you understand yourself and improve. Our next exercise for this chapter is to do a 360-degree evaluation for yourself in order to help clarify your definition of success.

Exercise 2.2

We've already done our fact-finding to see what other people think about their own success definitions. Now it's time to figure out what they think about *you*. Pick five people close to you, maybe the same ones you discussed success with or maybe others. Ask them: "Who do you think I want to be?" We all hope we're living the values we set out to, but are we demonstrating them to the people around us? How would your spouse and kids define you as a person, and does it match who you hope you are? When I talk to organizations, I often encourage an exercise where everyone takes out an index card and writes down the company vision. Inevitably, 50% of the cards converge pretty closely, 25% start to drift, and the last 25% are all over the map.

That's not good enough. It's certainly not elite.

What defines a group's success is convergence around one vision. We can take that back to the personal, too. What is your vision statement, and does everyone around you agree on it? This is the outward expression of the 3-by-5 card where you wrote your *who*. By asking people the question cold, without showing them your card first, you avoid steering the answers. You're not looking to validate what you've already done; you're looking to see how other people's perspectives about you hold up against how you see yourself.

What do we get from this? On the one hand, you don't want to let other people define you. You have to define yourself. On the other hand, you want to know what you are already putting out into the world, and if it matches what you expect. And getting this feedback—accepting it openly and learning from it—is a skill in itself.

As I said, feedback was an integral part of life as a SEAL, but a learning experience that really stands out for me is a feedback session when I was a White House Fellow. We were given all kinds of experiences as a Fellow, including exposure to leaders throughout the administration and an understanding of how the different parts of government work (and work together—or don't!). Perhaps one of the most impactful days was a media training workshop led by former White House Fellow Merrie Spaeth, the White House Director of Media Relations during Ronald Reagan's administration.

By then an outside consultant, Merrie came in and took us through an exercise where we were partnered up in teams of two. One of us was assigned to play the role of a government official and the other a reporter—at first, a friendly reporter, and then, in a second round, a hostile reporter. We switched roles back and forth, so we got to interview each other as friendly and as hostile. Everything was recorded on tape. We thought the interviews were the entire exercise, but then Merrie's team crafted two twenty-second audio clips out of our interview responses—one where we were made to look brilliant, and one where we were made to look as bad as possible. The lesson was that we should always imagine what the twenty-second clip that puts us in the worst possible light could look like, and to make sure that even at our worst, we were good enough to pass muster. There will always be supporters and detractors. "Make your detractors' jobs hard to do," I remember Merrie telling us. "Give them as little as you can."

That lesson has stuck with me. Sometimes when I speak in public and get asked a question I don't want to answer, I'll just say, *You all know I spent time in DC, so I know how not to answer the question I was asked. I'm instead going to answer the question I wish you'd asked.* Being honest and direct about that always elicits laughter.

The last part of the exercise was the one that made the largest impact. After a day of working together, of interacting and collaborating, and of interviewing each other, our partners were told to give us feedback on the things they thought we most needed to work on.

My partner was Sarita James, a brilliant graduate of Harvard and Oxford, a former Microsoft employee and McKinsey consultant, the head of economic development strategy for New York City under Mayor Bloomberg, and the leader of the US Small Business Administration's microloan program. She has since gone on to become a tech CEO helping students apply to college—and to financial aid programs to help them pay for it. Not incidentally, her bio calls her a "mission-driven tech CEO and government leader," and Mission Driven is a perfect way to describe her. I remember when I first met Sarita, she mentioned she had been a science fair kid who traveled around the country for national contests. I joked that she must not have been that good or she would have told me that she won. She looked at me, dead serious, and replied, "Oh, I did win—first place in the Intel International Science and Engineering Fair." In other words, Sarita is a rock star.

And she gave me some very tough feedback. "Sometimes when you're talking to me," Sarita said, "it seems like you are looking past me and surveying the room instead of locking in on our conversation. It can make me feel ignored, unimportant, and like you don't care."

I could have dismissed it or rationalized it. I mean, part of a Navy SEAL's nature is to always be scanning the room, hyper-observant to what's going on…but that's a defensive reply that doesn't acknowledge that it doesn't matter what you think you are communicating if the receiver is feeling something different. You can transmit anything you want, but the reception is what's important. I stopped myself from being defensive. I took the feedback and it has stuck with me ever since. I'm still not great at keeping myself from looking around, but I more frequently realize when I'm doing it. And I started noticing the same behavior in others. I saw how some people would be talking to you, and then as soon as someone more senior walked in the room, their head would snap and they would look for an escape. I never want to be that person, and Sarita's feedback has helped me immensely every day in life since then.

That's what good feedback can do. It can change you. And it should, if it's accurate and important. So in this exercise, listen to what people think of you. Press them on the areas where they think you need to improve. Question them on the things they say that don't match how you see yourself. Understand the gaps between who you think you are and how other people see you. They may notice qualities you don't recognize in yourself. Listen to those, and reflect on whether the people who know you best are understanding aspects of your *who* that you may be missing. They may also see correctable flaws, default behaviors, and raw instincts that are getting in your way. Do you like the answers you hear, or do you want to be someone else? What do you want them to say? And is what you feel yourself wanting people to say the very same thing as your definition of success?

FINDING THE PATH TO GET THERE

All of this thinking should help get you to a working definition of what success means for you. The next step is figuring out how to achieve it, while staying true to your *who*. I should be careful to be explicit about something: Your definition of success should and must change over time. Success isn't one destination, because you're never done achieving. Even if you solve the equation now, the world may change, your circumstances may change, and what drives you may change. You will still be you, the same *who* at the core of it all, but how that plays out practically should and will evolve. When I was in my twenties, success was being the best SEAL I could be, learning and growing and contributing to our missions. Now it's about broader impact, connecting people, making a difference, serving the Gold Star community, and lifting up as many of my fellow citizens as I possibly can.

Exercise 2.3

How do you get from where you are now to a place of success?

You look at where you're falling short, on a very granular level.

What is missing from your life that would make you successful? What are you doing that you shouldn't be doing? What are you not doing that you ought to be doing? A lot of us make to-do lists, but in this exercise I want you to make a to-don't list. What is holding you back? Where are you expending energy that could be better used to make a greater impact or get closer to reaching your definition of success?

On a business level, I ask audiences all the time, "Who's in charge of what you're not doing?" Nobody ever is, of course. But this works just as much on a personal level. Can you outsource the things that are wasting your time, or occupying too much of it? Do they even need to be done at all?

In *Never Enough*, I wrote about choosing the hard path. People often don't pick the hard path because they're afraid of being seen as failures. But by picking the hard path, either you end up right and happy because you've done something well or you end up learning something about yourself if you fail, testing your limits and understanding what is too much. You don't know if you can't do something unless you try. And in all cases, you learn.

By clearing things off your plate with a to-don't list, you create the room to do more, be more, and get better every day. The magic of compounding means that getting 1% better every day will allow you to achieve extraordinary things in the long run. I say that sometimes and people don't know how to put it into action. But think about it this way: If you write 1% of a book every day, you'll have a manuscript in a little over three months. If you lift 1% more weight every day, you'll be lifting almost three times more in that same time frame.

I think about my SEAL teammate Julio Fitzgibbons. He showed up to BUD/S training having literally never swum in his life. "You never swam?" I asked him later, incredulous, when he was in my platoon (and a great swimmer by then!). "Did you realize you showed up at Navy SEAL training, the most difficult swim training in the world?" Between swimming and drown-proofing, our instructors did things like tie our hands and ankles together and make us survive in the fourteen-foot deep end of a pool for an hour, then cross the entire pool without touching the bottom. Julio struggled with every exercise, always the last to finish but always passing. He did everything that was asked of him, and slowly, day by day, he got more comfortable in the water and grew his skills. He was probably the only person there with no experience in the water, but he made it through. I saw that grit and determination in every aspect of Julio's career; getting a little better every day makes you great.

I have more stories like Julio's—the military is full of people who are driven to get better. Staying in the water, we had an "exchange officer" from Singapore ("JG Teo"!) who thought he was coming to the States for a cushy Navy diving program and accidentally showed up instead at SEAL training. He was about 120 pounds soaking wet—and he was soaking wet the entire time he was there. But he also made it through.

In the next chapter, we're going to cover the meta-skills that can make you great—the attributes that will keep you moving forward and allow you to close the gap between your current state and the success you want to achieve. But before we get there, I want to close this chapter with one more exercise.

Exercise 2.4

What can you get better at? What is one thing you can do to make yourself 1% better—and can you do it every day? Depending on what you want to achieve, you'll probably want to make your own list, but here are some starting points: Three simple things I believe make me better every day. Perhaps they'll work for you as well. Do these, or others you choose, and you'll be able to move closer and closer to success, however you define it.

1. Flexibility: Lean over and let your body weight stretch you for two minutes, every single day. You'll be shocked how much closer to the floor you are in a month—and how much better your back feels.

2. Reconnection: Think of someone you haven't talked to in over a year and send that person a text saying they just popped into your mind, you hope they're doing well, and to make it a great day.

3. Hydration: Drink a glass of water as soon as you wake
    up, before eating or drinking anything else, and see
    how starting the day fully hydrated can help you.

Part of the point isn't to do any of these three things specifically, but to cultivate some kind of daily habit. Making yourself do anything every day is a form of discipline, and discipline is a big part of achieving any success. Certainly it was the foundation of SEAL training, and I think it's a foundation for life. George Washington once said, "Discipline is the soul of an Army. It makes small numbers formidable; procures success to the weak, and esteem to all." If it was good enough for our first president, it's good enough for me. No question, discipline is a start, and something we should all build on. Looking beyond that, there are other attributes to consider, and as you build your success tool kit, the meta-skills in the next chapter are the right place to turn.

CHAPTER THREE

The Meta-Skills That Matter

Madeleine Albright earned broad bipartisan respect throughout her diplomatic career, which culminated in her service as the first female Secretary of State in US history under President Clinton. Rising up the ranks to become a cabinet-level secretary seems like it would require a lifetime of planning and striving—starting as early as possible. Indeed, John Kerry, who served as Secretary of State under President Obama, was a nationally recognized activist who ran for Congress before his thirtieth birthday. Condoleezza Rice, Secretary of State under President George W. Bush, was already working in the State Department at age twenty-two.

Madeleine Albright, on the other hand, spent her twenties and thirties raising her children. Not that she wasn't brilliant and ambitious—she learned Russian to "pass the time" while her twin daughters, born six weeks premature, were in the neonatal ICU—but she was thirty-eight by the time she earned her PhD, and she didn't work in politics until she was nearly forty. A former professor recruited her to work in the West Wing a few years later, which began her rise to the government's highest foreign policy role.

That professor, Zbigniew Brzezinski, was President Carter's chief foreign policy adviser and had taught at Harvard and Columbia. He had plenty of distinguished students to choose from when he had the chance to bring someone into government. And yet he chose Albright. In chapter 9, I'll talk about how you don't need to—and in fact, you can't—do everything at once, and that you can be Mission Driven in different ways at different stages in your life—but the point I want to emphasize here is that Madeleine Albright accomplished what she did not because of her résumé—her *what*—but because of her *who*—the person she was, and the skills and gifts she had demonstrated as a student and as a human being.

I met Secretary Albright when I was a White House Fellow in a small group setting where we engaged in a true conversation. I asked her about her greatest professional disappointment in life, something she would do differently if she could. She gave a very specific and honest answer, about a 1996 interview she had done with *60 Minutes*, where she said that the bombing of children in Iraq had been "worth it." She regretted saying it, and she owned that it had been a big mistake. She said to us the greatest gift she could give was to ensure that we learned from her mistake: Never answer a question whose premise you don't agree with. Instead, stop to challenge the premise of the question. I didn't realize at the time that she had been asked about her biggest disappointment a hundred times already; it made it so much more impressive that she answered me with poise and care. She could have brushed the question off or, maybe worse, delivered her answer as a stock response. But it was clear she had thought deeply about this and was living with genuine regret that she'd ever said such a thing.

I saw Secretary Albright a number of times over the years at events or fundraisers, and even though she must have known a million people in Washington, DC, each time she acknowledged me and remembered me as the SEAL who'd asked her a hard question. She made me—and all the White House Fellows—feel like we were the next generation of leaders our nation needed, and I found her to be as kind, thoughtful, and sharp as her reputation. When I talk about meta-skills, I'm talking about the kinds of qualities that make someone look at you in the same light that I and so many others looked at Secretary Albright. I'm talking about the kinds of qualities that make you someone others want to pluck from obscurity and elevate, celebrate, and help. People with the right meta-skills get hired, get promoted, and become "overnight successes" that are rarely built overnight. They are the Mission Driven people who achieve what they set out to achieve and get to live their *who*.

WHAT ARE META-SKILLS?

At first glance, "skills" sounds like a résumé word. And yes, of course your skills matter when you're applying for a job or looking for a promotion. Employers expect that you can fulfill the requirements set out: experience in data analysis; comfort with digital marketing and SEO; expertise in HTML; anything the particular position might ask for. I'm not saying these kinds of skills are bad or shouldn't be built. By all means, if you want to program computers, you should learn Java or Python, and if you want to be a plumber, you should probably know how to install a sink. But these small-s skills only get you so far. There are always going to be people who seem, at least on paper, like they can do the very same things you can do. You do not get the job at the law firm merely because you have a law degree. These are the costs of entry.

Any great hiring manager—or anyone who's ever supervised anyone—knows that there is so much more to it. One hundred times out of a hundred, I would rather hire someone great who can learn sales, marketing, or security than someone mediocre who already knows it. I would rather bring someone terrific into an organization and teach them everything they need to master as opposed to settling for someone with exactly the right experience but the wrong attitude, the wrong work ethic, and the wrong state of mind.

I don't want to deny reality: Not every organization, and certainly not every hiring manager, does this in practice. In fact, I'd say that most organizations and people don't think this way. They need a red square, a yellow triangle, or a blue rectangle, and so they go and look for exactly that. Often they find it, but they leave plenty of other—perhaps far better—candidates on the outside looking in. I know lots of talented people who've experienced frustration at being unable to even get an interview at a place they think they want to work—or being treated with skepticism when their résumé doesn't match up. I think about my great friend Jon Fernandez, an MBA with an undergraduate degree in religion and more than a decade of experience in financial services I brought into VMware—a tech company, but not a tech guy. There was significant doubt about how well he'd fit. Three months later, the CEO told me, "I have to admit, I didn't think a profile like Jon's could succeed here, but he's one of the most effective people I've ever seen."

The most elite individuals and enterprises understand there is so much more to success than whether you've ever used Microsoft Office or installed a sink, or even whether you understand the relevant industry. They care more about fundamental attributes: Do you have the meta-skills to learn what you need, to navigate the organization, and to make an impact?

I have spent my private sector career seeking out those kinds of organizations and being open to those organizations seeking me. I had no experience in technology when I went to work for a tech company. I had no experience in government when I went to work in the White House. I had no experience in finance when I went to work for the world's largest asset management firm. I don't hide that, because it's not something to hide. I knew what I was bringing to the table, and so did the people who hired me. What I had was the ability to understand organizations and their missions; skill in identifying and motivating the people who individually needed to be excellent so that the collective team would be even more excellent; the vision to organize and lead teams to achieve challenging goals; the confidence that I could learn the specifics I needed in order to do the job (at times not many specifics at all—at the senior ranks of an organization, you're often making your greatest impacts at a big-picture level); and champions who were eager to make my case for me.

I get asked all the time about transitioning between industries and whether it's been challenging to have to learn an entirely new set of things. I firmly reject the premise of the question (thank you, Madeleine!). High-performing organizations are all very much the same, whether the SEALs, the White House, or a multibillion-dollar public company. The details are different, but what you have to do—think, plan, negotiate, strategize, commit—is identical. The skills the best people have are transferable no matter where they work and what they do.

You can—and must—build those skills in order to achieve your mission over the long run. Having the right set of meta-skills is what separates successful people from the ones who flounder and struggle and fail to find what they're looking for. Opportunities come to people who have the meta-skills in this chapter. These rock stars generate their own luck, and moments that initially seem like detours often end up leading to unexpected triumphs.

I wish I could say there's a magic six, twelve, or twenty-four meta-skills that you need to master, but the truth is that different people are wired to be great in different ways. Just like there is no single *who* we all aim to be, it would be an oversimplification to say there is one set of skills we all have to have. I'm about to dive into the five meta-skills I think are most important, and have shown themselves to have real value in *my* life, but I won't pretend this is an exhaustive set, or that each of us must embody every single one of these skills no matter our mission. Different skills can lead us to different places, and there may be a "secret sauce" you have that is not covered by this list. That's okay. Focus on the big picture: If you read the rest of this chapter and don't see yourself reflected in many of these skills, take a look in the mirror and ask yourself if something on this list might be what you're missing. Improving yourself in some of these areas may be exactly what you need to level up your life and achieve the impact you're after. Or if you think I've missed the most important meta-skill of all, write to me, help me learn what I'm missing, and you'll see it in my next book. Here we go:

META-SKILL 1: UNDERSTAND AND CREATE VALUE

If something you're doing isn't creating value—for someone, in some form—then it's hard for me to understand why you're doing it. This doesn't necessarily mean that everything we do has to create *monetary* value—it absolutely doesn't—but there needs to be some purpose to it, even if it's to recharge our batteries or enable us to be more prepared for a future circumstance.

The meta-skill here is to teach yourself to focus on how much value you're creating in any given moment and whether creating that value is the best and highest use of your time. If you're creating 1 unit of value, in any form, but something else you might be doing can create 100 units of value or 1000 units of value, then you may well be doing the wrong thing. The people who create the most value, no matter where that value comes from, will be the most rewarded in the end.

For instance, at VMware we engaged in a fundamental corporate transformation while I was there, moving from legacy perpetual software license sales (buy the product once and be done until you need to upgrade a few years later) to a software-as-a-service model (SaaS, where you pay an ongoing fee for what you're using, upgrades included as the products evolve). That's an extreme transformation. It involved changing the products (which all needed to be metered so customers could be billed for their consumption), changing how the sales team sold the products and got compensated for their

success, and changing operations to ensure the company was oriented to maximize customer value (thus maximizing shareholder
value in ways that could be reported accurately and transparently to
Wall Street every quarter). On top of these functional changes was
a culture shift that everyone needed to buy into: People needed to
think differently, prioritize differently, and execute differently. The
whole organization needed to be in tighter sync to understand the
sequence and flow of the transformation so the whole enterprise
could be more efficient.

One of the key groups we invested in was a forty-person team
that automated manual processes, moving repetitive, low-level tasks
from humans to artificial intelligence–powered "bots." But you
can't just automate bad workflows and expect good results. Before
you can have true digital transformation, you need to have analog
transformation, building the right processes first and only then
spending time and money automating them. The forty-person team
I'm talking about was charged with going around the organization
looking for the best processes and workflows to automate. The way
I guide teams in these business situations is to think about a 2-by-2
matrix with impact on one axis and effort on the other. You start
with the things in the "higher impact, lower effort" quadrant. Why?
You don't want to waste time doing hard things that don't yield
much impact, or even easy things that don't yield much impact.
It's relatively easy to convince people to stop doing the low-impact
tasks; what's harder is explaining that not all high-impact tasks are
created equal. If you can accomplish one hard high-impact task in
the time it takes to get through twelve easier tasks that each create
just as much impact, don't spend four years doing the hard one and

let the twelve easier opportunities slip away. Create the most value at the lowest cost.

The team spent its time looking for the arcane processes—the hard tasks—that could be made much easier. This did worry the people who performed those tasks. They feared they would lose their jobs. But my approach was always to reassure people that even if technology might be coming to take away human work, it was not going to take away humans. People who had underlying skills would always have more and different value-adding work to do.

Indeed, when I came to VMware, Pat Gelsinger, the CEO, sent an email to the company saying I was going to help us get to $20 billion in revenue and 50,000 employees, up from $14 billion in revenue and 40,000 employees. I called him and said I very much appreciated the note, but that real success would be to reach the same $20 billion in revenue but with half the current team—20,000 employees, not 50,000. That's not to say I wanted to fire 20,000 people. I wanted to take those additional 20,000 employees and get to even greater heights with them. My point was simply that I wanted to do more with less—and use our capacity to find new opportunities we weren't even thinking about.

One of the tricks to creating increased value is making sure you're focusing on strategy and not just tactics. Tactical work is often important—can you write that press release in an hour, or stuff those 600 envelopes by the end of the day?—but it is limited by your time and energy. There is only so much you can do, and to do double will take twice the time. Strategic work can add value in far more dramatic ways. Instead of thinking about how quickly you can write that press release, the strategic question is asking whether that's the right press release to be writing, or whether it should be a press release at all. It's about asking why the envelopes need to get stuffed, and if spending that same money in a different way would yield a far greater result. Rather than racing to get something done, ask whether it's the right thing to do, or whether it's worth coming up with a proposed alternative. Every decision we make has an opportunity cost. Can you be doing something better without sacrificing the goal?

A related question: How can you scale yourself and the work you are doing? You can't stuff ten times the number of envelopes—unless you reinvent the task and achieve the goal another way. If you had to do ten times what it is you do—how would you get it done? I think back to a mentorship program I helped create at VMware. The initial plan was for executives to be assigned one junior employee and spend twenty hours in one-on-one conversations with that employee. There is value in one-on-one conversations, for sure, but I asked myself how we could make better use of executive time and conveyed that if we could ask each executive to instead spend one hour talking to a group of twenty junior employees rather than twenty hours talking to only one of them, the program would cost each executive just one hour, and the junior employees would get exposed to twenty (or more) different executives. On top of that, by recording the sessions, we enabled future new hires to benefit from them. Said differently, moving from a one-to-one model to a one-to-many model added more exposure for the new hires and saved dozens of hours of executive time. What was rewarding was hearing compliments about some of those executives' sessions more than a year after they were recorded.

Your time is finite, and so the only way to make exponential progress toward a goal is to find a way to produce value that doesn't require you to personally touch every individual who might benefit. As I said, I can't help everyone personally become Mission Driven (and it would be impossibly hard to try): That's why I'm writing this book.

Another way to move from tactics to strategy is to diagnose problems down to the root cause. When something goes wrong, don't just think about the obvious reason, but consider why the error happened in the first place. The people who think this way—who don't just execute but look at the value they can create and work to create more—are the ones seen as leaders, the decision makers whose careers are worth investing in and whose missions are worth joining. When we debriefed after SEAL missions and examined something we could have done better, it wasn't enough to name what went wrong. We had to ask the person responsible: *Why? Why did you do that? What were you thinking?* It's only then that you get to the underlying issues and are able to fix problems so the errors ideally never happen again.

I should add the point that moving from tactics to strategy can sometimes scare people, who think they might end up coming up with ideas that could push them out of a job. Again, it's the same issue as technology replacing human work but not human beings. If your job is to stuff envelopes, and you think there's a better—and perhaps easier—way to create more value, you might naturally worry that, by proposing it, you're making yourself expendable. But if you are scared to innovate for your organization because you worry the innovation won't be properly valued, then you are, sadly, in the wrong organization. You should be celebrated for thinking strategically, and if you're pushed out for being too efficient, then you should feel secure in the idea that the right organization would never behave that way and would instead prize the meta-skill we're talking about here.

One final point: When we think about creating value, we sometimes ignore the value of our own time, and how we can make better use of it. We should all find opportunities to do the things we enjoy, certainly, but think about the trade-offs when it comes to things we don't enjoy. It may feel like a luxury, for example, to pay a service to do your laundry, but if doing your own laundry will prevent you from doing an extra two hours of work you can bill to a client for fifty times the amount of money the laundry costs, you are valuing your time quite poorly. It's like businesses that think they can cut spending down to the bone in order to increase profits. You can do a lot by cutting spending, but there's a limit—and to really move to the next level, you need to increase incoming revenue. Don't be afraid to bet on your ability to create value with time you can free up, rather than valuing your own time at nothing and wasting it on things you don't need to be doing.

META-SKILL 2: KNOW HOW TO INFLUENCE OTHERS

My best days while serving in Fallujah were when locals would come to us and tell us things that were going to save lives: "There's an IED [improvised explosive device] buried at the second tree around the bend," or "Be careful of the people in the house around the corner." There was nothing more valuable than information like that; in the case of an IED, we could find it, unbury it, disarm it, and make sure no one got hurt. These human intelligence victories—people on the other side deciding to reveal what they knew—came about because we spent a long time figuring out how to best influence the people around us. There is no one way to influence someone effectively. If you're trying to drive human behavior, you start with motivation. Some people are going to be motivated by doing the right thing; others will be motivated by money, or by a job. The more people you can find ways to appeal to, the more you get from them. I don't mean that in a calculated or transactional way, but winning people over is critical—whether in war or in business—and so the better you can do it, the more effective you will be.

Influencing others is a vitally important meta-skill to have. When you can influence the behavior of the people around you, you become someone who can get things done for the mission you're pursuing, organizational or personal. When you understand what motivates someone, you can drive their behavior to help you achieve your goals. There might be five people on a team, all driven by a different thing—one person wants credit, one wants money, one wants to learn, one wants time off, and one wants public recognition and praise. Knowing which person wants what helps you pull the right levers to create win-win situations where everyone gets what they're looking for. Conversely, knowing what frustrates people helps you stay away from those triggers.

Embedded within this lesson are three points. One is about political capital. When you understand what motivates someone, you can choose what to ask of them, and how to ask it. You can get people to want to do something rather than having to convince them or, if you're in a position to do so, to force them. You thus get things done without burning goodwill. When you don't choose wisely, you risk wasting that capital and having people resent helping you. In my graduate program at the Harvard Kennedy School, I took a class on negotiation. The definition I came away with was simple: Negotiation is the art of letting you have it my way. Two years after I graduated, I called my fantastic negotiation professor, Brian Mandell, and asked him to come lead a symposium for the SEALs. He said his price was $10,000. I jokingly replied, "I got an A in your class, so the price is zero dollars, and if you want to negotiate, let me know." (We paid his fee.) I wanted Brian to come in order to help my teammates gain this meta-skill. Typical SEAL training is basically "shoot, move, and communicate." But I wanted to broaden it out. SEALs are always negotiating overseas. We are advocates, diplomats, and peacemakers. Brian did a great job with the training, and our SEALs learned a ton about win-win negotiations and making everyone happy in the end.

The second point is about challenging the status quo. When you understand what drives people, you can push for change in constructive ways. There are companies, as just one example, that have junior team members listen in on calls in order to take meeting notes that they circulate to the team afterward. In the past, the need for this was a given—someone needed to take notes, or there wouldn't be a record of what was said. Technology—artificial intelligence, in this case—has massively changed the landscape. There may still be value in having junior employees listen in and write down what's happening, as a learning opportunity and to get to know the language of the business. But if there are better ways to learn, or if the learning isn't the point—it's just about the meeting notes—then the practice can be reconsidered. There may be more efficient ways to use the time and create value.

"We do it this way because we've always done it this way" is a completely unsatisfactory explanation for anything. Rites of passage that don't have a greater justification are frankly stupid. An example: In SEAL training, one of the ways we were pushed out of our comfort zone was with an exercise known as rock portage. When there's a super-high surf, with massive waves, the instructors adjust the schedule and put "rock portage" on the schedule. We get into a rubber boat in shorts, T-shirts, and WWII-era life jackets ("ka-poks") and paddle out from the famous rock jetty outside the Hotel Del Coronado, trying to get beyond the surf zone (where the waves stop breaking and become giant swells), and then turn around and try to get the boat back to the jetty, riding the waves, working our hardest not to tip over. In practice, we end up spewing men, paddles, and boats onto the rocks, then carrying the boat over those rocks doing "land portage," where every step is begging for a broken bone or a cracked skull.

It's a simulation of needing to bring a boat to shore in harsh conditions on foreign "soil" that is really just pure rocks. Hopefully you're never in that situation, but if you are, you need to know you can do anything in the worst of conditions. They make the training situation as hard as possible, and trust me, you are quickly exhausted as the boat bashes you into the rocks again and again. Back when I was in training, people would hit their heads every so often and be knocked out of the class for days, weeks, or forever. This was pointless. It was a simulation and the skills being developed had nothing to do with risking a head injury. So now they wear helmets. Some old-school SEALs criticize the change, saying the new trainees have it easy. But no, it's not easier; it's smarter.

I don't know who advocated for the change, and how they made it happen—but clearly, whoever it was had the meta-skill of being able to exert influence effectively, even in a rigid institution like the military. Change can work in different ways in different organizations, and figuring out how to appeal to people is critical. Challenging authority to advocate for change in the SEALs—sometimes with a great deal of volume and intensity—was very different from doing so in the White House Situation Room, where the same kind of approach would not have been appreciated.

The third point here is about communication. Communication is about more than just the concrete outputs we typically associate with people who work in a communications role—website content, white papers, etc. Communication is about being able to effectively transmit your thinking process. And it's a critical meta-skill no matter your job. To wit: If asked to list the kinds of skills a SEAL needs, most people would land on a few predictable answers—strength, agility, calm intensity, focus. Which is why my teams were sometimes confused when I'd sit them down on a day when the weather was keeping us from training and I'd give each SEAL a topic. "Take the next two minutes to prepare a two-minute speech on this subject," I'd say.

"Public speaking?" they would ask, incredulous. Why did they need to work on public speaking? It made no sense to some of them, until I explained it on two levels. First, at some point all SEALs will have to represent themselves and their unit to people in the community or to leaders we might have to interact with. Just like they needed negotiation skills, they also needed to be able to express themselves well, in case I or another leader was unavailable and the responsibility fell to them. Second, becoming a better speaker is really about becoming a better thinker, organizing thoughts and defining goals—and that is a skill that transfers to everything we do.

The best communicators have a tightness of thought. They set goals at the beginning of a meeting, to put everyone on the same page. They stay focused on the mission. They avoid needlessly wasting other people's time. We've all been in rooms where someone starts vacuuming up attention needlessly by asking a question that either never gets to the question mark or is being asked for a self-indulgent purpose rather than focused on the end value. This is a communication problem (also sometimes an attitude problem, another meta-skill we'll look at in a moment), and if you are the one being stared at by a bunch of people who feel like you're wasting their time, you're doing something wrong. There's an age-old saying in the SEAL Teams, where platoons are made up of sixteen men: "When fifteen men are wrong, look in the mirror." It may well be that you are failing to influence in a positive, effective way.

In my public speaking exercise, all the SEALs listening gave feedback to the presenters, just like we did after missions. The feedback was another way to make us all better.

META-SKILL 3: NEVER STOP LEARNING

It is easy to grow complacent—but you can't if you're striving to be Mission Driven. There are two components to this meta-skill. The first is to start with foundational learning and build your way up. When you enter a new space, you should be trying to learn everything you can as quickly and efficiently as possible. The second point is to push yourself to learn harder and harder things. I made the point in *Never Enough* that the best of us lean into challenges and aren't afraid to be uncomfortable. This applies to learning as much as anything. It is tempting to stay within your comfort zone, but the meta-skill I look for in people I hire or partner with on a project is that they always want to know more.

I think about my former SEAL teammate Jimmy Graham, who devoted time on his own to training as a radio operator, learning about the different antennas and wavelengths to use on our missions...and eighteen months later saved our lives because he knew exactly how to call for help in a crisis. Or I think about two brave SEALs, Bo Reichenbach and Chris Serle, who I "volun-told" to spend time on a day off learning in the base camp's medical center instead of playing Xbox—barely any time at all before they were blown up during a mission and found themselves in that very same medical facility...able to understand and appreciate what was going on to save their lives because they had taken that time to learn. I'm still haunted by Bo's screams—"Mr. Hayes, please put me out now! PLEASE put me down now!" and then a few minutes later having to amputate Bo's leg, all while moving back and forth to look into Chris's explosion-blackened face trying to help him, imagining there was no chance he was ever coming back to us. Chris, in fact, ended up recovering and going to medical school—and becoming a doctor after leaving the SEALs. The reality is that I think about those situations and realize how lucky I am to be here on this planet, and that gratitude is part of what keeps me wanting to grow and learn, too, and share and help others.

In my current role at Insight Partners, I meet a large number of C-suite leaders. Their jobs are typically very intense. When people leave those roles, they are faced with the question of what to do next. Some want more of the same, no question. They want to go to a bigger company, potentially move up to the CEO role if they weren't there already, and continue to be a corporate leader. Others are looking for something very different. They still want to keep learning, but they don't necessarily want the deep responsibility and pressure. They can do many different things. They can become advisers to multiple companies or organizations; they can serve on boards; they can find roles where they will coach and mentor. When I talk to them down the line, the difference between the ones who are satisfied and the ones who are frustrated isn't about the size of the job, the compensation, or the power. CEOs sometimes get bored; consultants sometimes get bored, too. The ones who don't get bored are the ones who have kept on learning. The executives who made their choices with an eye toward being challenged, in a position where they could keep growing even if the growth looked different than it used to, are the ones who are most content and still feel like they are driving forward with a mission.

What gives most of us energy is that growth—so the more of it we can do, the better. And the more we learn ourselves, the more we can help others learn, too.

META-SKILL 4: BUILD COMFORT WITH THE UNKNOWN

If you have all the answers, that usually means the questions weren't hard enough. And yet so many people are paralyzed by ambiguity and don't know what to do when things are uncertain. Being able to not just manage through uncertainty but thrive in it is a meta-skill that serves people well no matter the context. Whether it's an emergency situation or just a point in time when a decision needs to be made without full information, the people who can grapple effectively, use what they know, learn what they can, and take appropriate risks when it comes to the unknown are the ones who succeed.

There were so many moments of uncertainty as a SEAL. You have to be comfortable standing in front of a room and saying, "I don't know exactly what's going on, but here's what we're all going to do about it." There is always a smart next step, even while you're waiting for more information. You can go a level up and think about what you can do to get the information you need, or you can look to the future and think about the things that will need to happen in the aftermath, no matter what is going on right now.

I think back to when I was guest lecturing at Harvard Business School and running the class through a case study about a Swedish travel company, Fritidsresor, that lost a bunch of tourists during the 2004 Indonesian tsunami. It's four in the morning, you're the CEO of a tourism company, and you get a phone call: There has been a massive tsunami, and almost a quarter of a million people are dead, some of them your customers. Many more are trapped in the region, at risk. You have no idea what is going to unfold. You're a small company. You've never been through anything like this before. You have no crisis plan. What do you do?

The first few answers I got from the class were all about reporting steps: Tell the board; come up with messaging for the unavoidable media onslaught; call a meeting to figure out how this happened and why there wasn't a plan in place. Put a plan in place for next time, sure. All things that will have to be done, of course. But none of them solves the real problem: There are people still trapped there, worried families, lots of uncertainty. You don't know what is going to unfold, but if you take a step back, you realize there's only one question to answer: What will make this situation better? And the answer is getting the people out of there, as many as you can, as quickly as you can, while at the same time thinking about how the situation will likely become worse and how you need to get more resources to prepare for any challenging new information you will potentially learn in the next day—or the next minute.

The CEO in this case called the Swedish government—but they were as flat-footed as everyone else, and did not have a plan to help. What next? The company ended up becoming one of the heroes of the tsunami rescue effort. They evacuated almost 5,000 Scandinavians from the region—some of them customers, many of them not. They arranged for charter planes, airlifting group after group, with their local staff organizing the effort. This cost a ton of money. They were entirely unprepared to do it. But the CEO and his staff did not shrink in that moment of crisis. They stepped up and managed through the frightening uncertainty. We should all strive to react in similar fashion.

A related point here is about knowing the difference between useful knowledge—information that turns unknowns into knowns—and extraneous information. This has another name: differentiating signal from noise. I was at a board meeting recently where we spent two hours discussing a number of issues, none of which were particularly critical to the organization's future. I spoke up at the end, and said, "This didn't feel like the highest and best use of the past two hours," and I suggested we make an agenda for the next meeting that would cut down on the wasted time. It is easy to accept two hours of pleasant uselessness, but that doesn't move an organization forward. Being able to identify what's important and what isn't—and making sure you are engaging in activities that reduce ambiguity and create more knowledge—can be hard, but it's a meta-skill worth growing.

META-SKILL 5: BE INTENTIONAL ABOUT YOUR ATTITUDE

The final meta-skill to discuss here is about your approach to life. The other four meta-skills are largely about knowledge: Do you know how to think strategically, how to influence others, how to collect the right information? But this last one is more internal, about the point of view you bring to the table. There are five components to the right attitude—four of which I'll discuss here, and then the last one, which is so important and fundamental that it gets its own chapter, comes next.

The first component is about agility, and a willingness to adjust to the situation. Just like you have to understand that different people are driven by different motivations in order to exert influence effectively, you need to realize that different circumstances may require something different from you. You need to be able to be someone different at different times. I look at my friend Denis McDonough as a perfect example of this. He is the former White House chief of staff for President Obama and Secretary of Veterans Affairs for President Biden. He had just come off the Obama campaign when I was a White House Fellow, and had never worked in the White House before. He quickly realized there is a difference between what you do to optimize winning an election and what you do when you have to govern. It is said that politicians must "campaign in poetry and govern in prose." But how do you do that? How do you get things done when we have a two-party system where people seem so far apart in so many ways? Once you have to govern, the options narrow from the plans and promises you made on the campaign trail. Some things simply can't get done. But there is no use wallowing. You need to roll up your sleeves, pivot to what *is* possible, and do it.

I was a rare person at my level in government who lived through the transition from George W. Bush to Barack Obama. Many director-level professionals were political appointees who went home. As a White House Fellow, I was able to stay in my role. National security doesn't care about election cycles, and crises emerge just about every day. People like Denis had to come in and hit the ground running, working within the realities of the system to make President Obama's vision come true. Denis was a master at knowing how to pull the right levers and marshal all the tools in his tool kit to make things happen—who to turn to for what, how to inspire, how to spread information, down to which reporters he needed to call in order to get the right messages out to the world. He succeeded because he didn't let himself become beleaguered by what couldn't get done; he had the attitude that change was possible, and so he always engineered it and impressively never let anything get in his way.

The second component of attitude is resilience. When things don't go our way, we can lose hope—but that's exactly the point when we need to push forward and think of new approaches. We can't fear failure. How well you do the work after a failure is what determines whether you will fail next time or succeed. You can't run from failure. You need to be honest, recognize areas where you could have done better, and reflect on what should be done differently next time. I told the story in *Never Enough* about a SEAL mission in Kosovo where we were compromised—the enemy knew we were watching them—and the commanding officer chose to go ahead with the mission anyway. We ended up shot at, actively hunted, and barely made it out alive. Fifteen years later, as the commanding officer, this time in Afghanistan, I saw a similar pattern emerging. I canceled a seventy-two-hour mission after the first day because I believed we had been detected. The risk was not worth the reward. But I had the courage to do it only because I had revisited our failure in Kosovo again and again, internalizing the lessons and accepting that we never should have been put in that position.

The third component is intentionality with your emotions. Dr. Shannon Kula Clark, the chief of staff whose funeral I described in chapter 1, had true intentionality when it came to how she expressed her feelings. That was how she got things done. She was ferocious in her objective, and yet so kind to everyone she encountered. Too often we think that to get things done, we have to raise our voice and make ourselves impossible to deal with. That's not how the most successful people operate (or at least not how they ought to). In ten months in command in Afghanistan, in the most extreme and trying of times, I raised my voice exactly twice at my staff. And neither time was it driven by the passion of the moment. Both times, I told my second-in-command exactly what I was planning to do and why. My elevated tone was intentional—to drive my team to push harder, because I believed in the moment they needed that kind of emotion from me. Think about when your parents yelled at you, out of control themselves, as compared to when they calmly explained how you could have done something better. Which technique was more effective?

Part of intentionality is knowing when to lighten the mood, too. I think back to Julio Fitzgibbons, the nonswimmer from chapter 2. He was a master of finding just the right practical joke to get us all laughing and out of our own heads. I remember when he taped me in my hammock and smeared peanut butter all over me while I was sleeping—which, deep in the jungle of Panama, is no laughing matter ("50 caliber" ants, howling monkeys, and spiders the size of your face!).

Finally, work ethic. Beyond all of these meta-skills is our willingness to perform, even when it's hard. I tell new SEALs that until they learn the strategic and tactical skills they are going to need on the job, all they have is their attitude and their work ethic. Show up with the drive, hunger, and curiosity to work—and you will be rewarded.

When people tell me they're worried about someone else's work ethic—or even their own—it's often a pretty easy problem to solve, because I don't think most people are lazy at their core. We all want to accomplish things—we all want to be Mission Driven. What makes us lazy is that we're not doing the *right* things. We're either not working on things that inspire us or we don't understand the pain we have to push through now in order to get to embark on the larger mission that will energize us later. If we saw the path clearly, maybe we could be more passionate about the not-fun stuff needed to get there. After all, if we knew that working hard would be guaranteed to get us the life we wanted, each of us would gladly sign up.

So if you feel uninspired or unmotivated, it probably isn't a work ethic problem. It's either a problem with the goal, or with your ability to map your current action back to that goal.

When I was talking to Dan Hurley's basketball team at UConn, we dove into exactly this point: Once you're clear about the goal, working hard shouldn't be a problem. No athlete at that level needs to be reminded about hard work. "What price are you willing to pay to win?" I asked. For a pro, it has to be everything.

I provoked the team further, asking them to think about the person on their team they like the least (though not to say the name out loud!). "Seriously—who is the last person on the team you want to hang out with in your free time?"

No matter how tight a team is, there has to be an answer to that question.

"And when that person calls you and asks for help, what is your reaction?"

The only way to be elite is to be fully committed to even that person. That person shouldn't have to finish their sentence before you answer, "Yes, of course I'll help—how?" Elite teams don't win only because they can shoot, dribble, and pass better than everyone else. They win because they know they're limited only by work ethic and imagination. They win because they are a true team, made up of true teammates. It's culture that wins championships. UConn teammates Andre Jackson, now a shooting guard with the NBA's Milwaukee Bucks, and Adama Sanogo, now a power forward with the Chicago Bulls, called me the night before UConn's championship game and told me that message—of giving it all for every one of your teammates—is what resonated with the team all season long. They went on to win the championship game and excitedly cut the nets down to celebrate a victorious year.

If you're not feeling the same motivation they were, you need to figure out the problem. To diagnose a lack of energy around a goal can take some thinking. How important to you is what you're trying to do? And if you don't feel like it's important, why not? Go back to your *who* and figure out if this simply doesn't fit. If it's important, why aren't you motivated? Are there choices you can make to fix the problem? Are you distracted by something else, either something that can't help but be distracting (health, family, etc.) or by habits (sleep, addiction, social media) that you can and absolutely should change?

The meta-skill is not simply to accept that your work ethic is failing you, but to diagnose the problem and fix it.

SO HOW DO YOU BUILD THESE META-SKILLS?

It's easy for me to tell you the skills you need. But how do you build them? The answer is focused practice.

Exercise 3.1

Pick a meta-skill—one that I've mentioned here, or a component of one, or another meta-skill that emerges from your own hard thinking. Make it one you wish you were stronger at (and if you think you're strong at all of them, then I'm picking for you, and it's the meta-skill of humility). We all have places where we can improve. I'm impatient, as I've already mentioned, and that can bleed through into my attitude at times. I'm working on it, exactly as I suggest you work on a skill here.

Going back to the principle behind Exercise 2.4—1% better!—this is something you can get a little better at every day. Take your selected skill and imagine you were creating a training course to teach it to someone else. What exercises would you have them do? What situations would you put them in? What would you ask of them in order to prove they had mastered it? Having created the course—do it yourself. Each day, spend a few minutes in focused practice growing your meta-skill. Once satisfied, pick another one. You will soon be a master at all of them.

There is one more attitude component that I said deserves its own chapter. I've left it to stand by itself because it's even more than a meta-skill—not that the meta-skills in this chapter aren't critical attributes for success. Rather, it's what I think of as a fundamental orientation toward the world—and the key to every success I've experienced and seen in the world, without question. Truly successful people are driven by one thing above all else: They want to help. And they soon discover that helping others does help others…but it ends up helping *themselves* even more.

CHAPTER FOUR

Helping Others Helps Us More

Perhaps the person who made the single largest defined impact on my life was Fred Kacher, a White House Fellow two years before me, who didn't need to spend an hour on the phone with me selflessly offering advice about how to navigate the White House Fellow application process, but his sixty minutes of finely tuned wisdom likely made the difference between me getting chosen or not.

Fred told me three things. First, be yourself. He told me I could write what I wanted in the essays, but at some point, if I made it to the national finals (thirty-two from a field of thousands), I would undergo three days of questioning from the hardest judges trying to figure out who I really was. The White House Fellows community values integrity above all else. He emphasized: *Don't be one thing on paper and another in real life.*

Second, he told me to think about how I wanted to impact the world, and to work backward from there to figure out what I wanted from the Fellowship. How to impact the world has since become the animating question of my life, and certainly the animating question of this book. I can't say it was Fred who set me on the course of being Mission Driven—that instinct was in place long before—but certainly he was one who helped me start to articulate it and understand it.

Third, he asked me to imagine I was a judge, choosing the people to be selected. The program gets to pick only fourteen people in the country each year. He asked me what types of people I would pick, and why. And then, he told me to work backward from there to make sure I was one of them.

What was special about Fred is that someone I only shared a mutual friend with was so generous as to jump on the phone and not just give me three minutes of advice so he could check the "I helped" box, but to give me a thoughtful hour that has stuck with me ever since. Fred cared.

Fred lives his life in a Mission Driven way—and it is no accident that as I write this, seventeen years after that call, he is a vice admiral in charge of the Navy's Seventh Fleet. Thanks to Fred's phenomenal advice, my selection as a White House Fellow led to the most formative year of my life. And what Fred didn't know is while I intently listened to and learned from him, I was also studying him and deciding that he represented exactly the type of person I wanted to be around, learn from, contribute to, and impact the world with. I wanted to get the chance to meet a lot more Freds. The line I remember most from my application was from the 200-word essay that had the prompt "Why do you want to be a White House Fellow?"

My response boiled down to this: "I don't just want to positively impact people; I want to positively impact people to positively impact others. That nonlinear, exponential good in the world is what I seek."

That's what we're doing here, and while I'm writing this to help you, and to help you help others, in the end you are also helping me by reading it. You are allowing me in, allowing me to guide you, allowing me to create the impact I am after. I don't know what will emerge from this book for you, and I don't know what will emerge from this book for me, but I do know this: People like Fred are a gift, and they understand the premise of this chapter. Helping others helps others—sure, that's a given. But helping others ends up helping you even more. It helps you reach your *who*. It helps you drive the change you want to see in the world. It helps you have impact.

My conversation with Fred was just one conversation. There are countless others who had a lifetime of impact on me through their own selfless choices. I think about my grandfather, my Bumpa, who didn't talk much about what it was like to be at Pearl Harbor that fateful morning, and then become a naval aviator, leading a bomber squadron out of the Aleutians. When he did open up in his late eighties, he shared how he prayed every day not just for his teammates but for the enemy as well. As he grew older, he told me that he asked for forgiveness for the lives he ended while simultaneously not torturing himself over it, because he knew he had a job to do and did his best to be the best he could be. As I've grown older, I think back on that conversation because I experience the same thing. I wasn't a pilot, but as a SEAL commander in Iraq and Afghanistan, I made decisions to execute or cancel operations, and was the single person to decide whether and when to authorize pilots to drop bombs on targets during operations. We lived much the same life, two generations and wars apart. One of the things that sticks with me the most was when my grandfather told me how he'd lived some very hard days. And that the only thing to do when you're having a hard day is go find someone who is having a harder day and help them.

I do my best to repay Fred by helping others the way he helped me, and I've talked to perhaps a hundred White House Fellow applicants behind me. I've already mentioned the mortgages I've paid off for Gold Star widows, and while I only do what I do to help these women whose families paid the ultimate sacrifice, what they may not realize is that I walk away from those conversations and moments even more rewarded than they are.

There are always ways to help, and ways to find that kind of reward. For instance, I get calls with some frequency from head-hunters about potential roles, and there's little I like more than being able to give them the name of someone better than me. You might be thinking that sounds a little less selfless than the other examples, and that's true—there are benefits for me from building trusted relationships with headhunters and job seekers alike, being someone they think to call when they have big opportunities. One of those roles, one day, may be the right one for me, and to have the chance to compete for it might be exactly what I want. But that's part of the point of this chapter: We don't have to be selfless to help other people, and it doesn't matter all that much whether we think we're being selfless or not. The other people still get helped. It's the help that matters, and everyone I've seen have standout success in life, I believe without exception, has been someone who shares the orientation to jump in and give. Your first instinct when asked to do something should be to think, "Is there any way I can do this?" And your answer, far more times than not, should be "yes."

HELP FORMALLY; HELP INFORMALLY

Or the subhead for this section could be: "Don't Just Be a Mentor; Be a Teammate." There's a better framing for the question I just suggested you ask yourself. Asking yourself if there's a way you can help, after your help has already been requested, is important, sure. But if all you're doing is helping the people who ask for it, you're not helping nearly enough. Having a helping mindset is not just reactive. Too many of us look for formal permission to help or wait until we're invited into the lives of others. But there are an infinite number of opportunities to help without being asked. And those opportunities allow you to bring your own mission to the table rather than just supporting someone else's. In exactly that spirit, no one asked me to start paying off widows' mortgages, but it was an idea I felt strongly about. As a SEAL, I worked to get companies to donate money to fund free babysitting hours for mothers and fathers at home while their husbands or wives were deployed overseas. No one asked for it, but I saw the need. And I have to tell you, fundraising for that program led to me being asked to speak at a big conference for Goldman Sachs, where, thanks to that speech, I ended up being offered a job when I was leaving the SEALs. That would not have happened otherwise. Helping others helped me more.

Along similar lines, formal mentorship relationships can be terrific, without a doubt, and I know plenty of people who have

benefited from mentor-mentee coaching, or the top-down part-
nership that often takes place between a manager and someone
at a different level in an organization. But to silo the help you give
into formal structures misses out on all the other opportunities we
have to benefit other people and make a difference in ways large and
small. In the workplace, why wait to be assigned a mentee? Find one.
Or two. Or twelve. Help is help, and the more of it we can provide,
the better off everyone will be.

In that spirit, it may sound unexpected coming from someone
who spent a good part of his career in the military, but I hate to see
hierarchy rear its head when it comes to help and service—and service, by the way, takes many forms, and I don't just mean military
service. Yes, it may well be part of the job description for a person
to help the people who outrank them in an organization—but it
ought to be in everyone's job description to help up and down the
hierarchy, with far less regard for titles than some people maintain.
I often begin my work emails with the word *Teammates*, because
the best workplaces really are teams, where everyone pitches in to
assist each other. We all play *different* positions—not higher-value
or lower-value, not more or less important, just different. And it's
quite often the most junior people on the team who are doing the
real work for the organization. I sometimes go so far as to joke, "I
don't work here, I just talk about the work." It's the people executing
who are so often the most critical.

I cringe when I see senior leaders assuming they know better. I
aspire to be the opposite—to revel in the opportunity to enlist the
help of people with skills I lack, and I never miss the opportunity to
thank them for being good at things I cannot do.

WORK IS A FAMILY—OR AT LEAST IT CAN BE

Adam Grant (who generously shared his own lessons with me as I wrote *Never Enough*) talks about how work isn't family; family is family. I respect Adam immensely, but in some ways I disagree. No, work isn't the same kind of family as the one you have at home, with what we hope is unconditional love and deep, everlasting bonds, but it ought to be a family of some kind nonetheless, where we know we can count on the people around us. Beyond the transactional relationship of working for money, we should see our work, to the degree possible, as a joint mission, being performed with people we genuinely care about, respect, and want to support.

Once a job is reframed as a mission, it becomes easier to embody the kind of orientation that I'm talking about in this chapter. Success in the professional sphere requires commitment, often with even more time spent at work than with our actual family. It also requires a mindset of focusing on the bigger picture beyond just your own siloed role. If people at work know they can count on you, and you know you can count on them—to step up as needed, without worrying about credit or the specifics of job responsibilities—then the organization winds up better.

Our work lives and home lives are more blended than ever before, and while it's easy to bemoan the loss of work-life balance and a true separation between those spheres, I prefer to see it as less of a binary. Our work and our personal life both need to track back to our *who*, and being Mission Driven doesn't just mean Mission Driven at work or Mission Driven at home. It means understanding that there is a convergence. We are one person in all contexts and in all facets of life, and that one person needs to be no less committed to help and support in either dimension.

I am not saying we should let work intrude on family time when it doesn't have to, or we shouldn't strive to unplug and recharge as necessary. Instead, we should realize the simple truth that the more our workplace feels like a Mission Driven enterprise, the more we like and trust the people we work with, and the more we extend an orientation of helpfulness to everything we do, the more fulfilled we will ultimately be.

I KNOW, BUT...

It's easy to think of objections to almost everything I've written in this chapter so far. A few of them:

- Doesn't an eager willingness to help mean you might be taken advantage of?
- Won't putting the team first risk that you won't be recognized for your individual contributions?
- Why should you do free work that isn't in your job description, especially when you know that many companies show little loyalty to even their best employees?
- Doesn't "helping" eat up time you could otherwise be spending with your family—your *real* family, not your work family—or putting in the effort to find new and even better opportunities?
- And if you're always helping others, how are you ever getting your real work done—the work you're getting

paid for—and trying to be promoted, learn more, and earn more?

These are all perfectly valid but, to me, miss the point entirely. If someone gave you the opportunity to hire a friend or a colleague, right now—who do you turn to first? The person who constantly says "No, sorry, I can't," or the person who always steps up to help? The person keeping a tally of their contributions to be sure they get appropriate credit, or the one who's happy to pitch in for the greater good? The one who refuses to be reached after hours, or the one who's there when needed?

Life is a balance. Of course you want to be recognized for the work you do and maintain high visibility across an organization. Of course you don't want to constantly feel overstretched and like you never have any time off. You don't want to feel like you're being taken advantage of. You have to use your time wisely and get creative with the ways you help. (You don't have to take every call; instead of one-on-one meetings, maybe you should write a book!) But you also have to trust a few things:

First, related to the question of credit and recognition, is that good businesses realize that responsibility and accountability should grow together. When it's time to figure out who should get more responsibility, it is essential to look beyond the loudest or most visible people to the ones who are driving success. Great leaders know that it's not about face time; it's about impact. I wrote in *Never Enough* about how the L in SEAL stands for lazy, but it shouldn't just be SEALs; it's everyone. And I don't mean lazy as in sleeping all day and never doing any work. It's about finding the most efficient path to the goal. Often that efficiency involves acting as a cog in someone else's wheel and not trying to be the entire machine yourself. When I look for who to promote, I ask their peers. You want to be the one your teammates hold up as critical to good outcomes, whether or not you have greater visibility beyond the people you work directly with. When someone like me asks the team who stepped up, be the one they point to.

If that doesn't resonate in your organization or your line of work, and if leadership is incapable of looking beyond the loudest voices, that's a business problem, and maybe an organization you should be looking to leave—*not* a reason to give up and stop trying to help.

Okay, okay—you're still pushing back, aren't you? You don't think I'm living in reality, where efforts are ignored and the wrong people get moved up in the ranks for all kinds of wrong reasons. Sure, injustices happen. Part of why I left the SEALs was that in our annual fitness reports—our yearly evaluations—we are ranked against the others in our role. There were five commanding officers in my peer group. Our boss had to rank us 1 to 5. The top person would be called an EP, for "early promotion." The second would be MP, for "must promote." The others are all possible to promote, but not guaranteed. I had always been an EP in every competitive annual report for my entire career. I was given the EP ranking once again, and my report was signed. A day later, I received a call from my boss. "Mike, I need to make a change," he said. "Your record is so strong that I have no doubt you will be selected for Major Command [the next level up], but [the other guy] doesn't have the combat record you have, so he needs this. I'm trying to get two people promoted here."

He switched me to the MP. And while I understood what he was trying to do—and my peer who got the EP ranking was a superb SEAL, leader, and human being—it made me frustrated, and still makes me frustrated, because it felt like all of my hard work and my commitment to being the best was dismissed and ignored.

Maybe that sounds petty. Maybe I would have been selected for Major Command regardless. Maybe I wouldn't have been. But we want life to feel like a meritocracy. We don't want to feel underappreciated. I decided that day that I would leave the SEALs after my combat deployment to Afghanistan commanding SEAL Team TWO. Is this the advice I'd give someone else? Not exactly. We shouldn't make decisions driven by emotion. But I am human. I react like anyone else. This was an injustice, and I still think I was right to want to leave the organization, but there's a different lesson I should have taken, and that I understand when I look back now: Things may not work out in the short run, but in the long run, I promise they do. I've seen it, time and time again. My situation may not be the most dramatic example of workplace injustice, but it felt like it to me at the time—and what I walk away with is this: Taking all the emotion out of it, the right answer was never going to be to sacrifice my values and character and settle for being less than great. It was to find a different place to be great.

When I told my boss I was leaving the SEALs, he was truly shocked. He backpedaled and tried to talk me out of it, because he didn't think I would make the decision I did. But as satisfying as it might have been to hear him recoil, I tried very hard not to lean into those positive emotions and not to feel smug about making someone uncomfortable after they'd made what I thought was a bad decision. That doesn't mean you can't tell an organization you're leaving because of something you aren't happy with. But your goal, ultimately, doesn't have anything to do with the organization or how your decisions make anyone else feel. Your goal has to be about you and your own path to being Mission Driven. You have to do your best to make logical, rational, emotionless decisions that help you achieve what you're aiming for.

It won't always be perfect, and sometimes, taking emotion out of it, the right decision might be to stay in an organization and make the best of it. Will you feel like a sucker sometimes, a person who gets taken advantage of? Perhaps. But you're not the sucker if you learn from it. No matter the circumstance, you ask yourself what you can gain from the experience, and what clues you saw that might prevent the same thing from happening next time. Maybe there were signals. Maybe there weren't. In either case, you make the best of a disappointing situation and understand your main job is to put yourself in the best situation for you, whether that's staying or leaving, pushing or taking a step back and letting things go.

The other thing we have to understand is related to time. Time often feels more finite than it is. Impact doesn't always have to steal energy from work or family. We don't need to see giving as something that takes a toll on us in terms of time and effort because sometimes it really doesn't. There are very easy things we are in unique positions to do that can make a real impact in almost no time.

Recently the son of one of my teammates, Jason Lewis, who was killed in Iraq on our deployment in 2007, called me. He was a junior in college, seeking advice on finding an internship. This is an easy lift for me. I spent fifteen minutes on the phone with him, and then made some introductions. He's a great kid; his father was a friend and a national hero. He'll end up with an internship that might change the course of his life, and it took almost no effort from me.

I tell this story for another reason: I can frame what I did in a couple of different ways. I can say I was asking for a favor in order to help a young man find an internship, but the better way to think about it is I was helping to make it super-easy for a friend of mine to help someone in need by hiring this great kid as an intern. I helped two people at once.

While we sometimes feel awkward asking for professional favors, if we're feeling awkward, it's probably because we're either asking for the wrong thing or approaching it incorrectly. We need to step outside of ourselves and think about value. I wasn't asking for a favor. I went through my mental Rolodex of contacts and really thought about who that young man could help. What were his skills and interests and where could he really add value? For the people I reached out to, it wasn't just that I was asking for a favor, and it wasn't just that I was making it easy for them to help someone. There was another benefit: I was delivering someone of value to a business that needed their help. If you can bring someone something of value, then all of a sudden you're not asking for help; you're giving.

This is value creation—and it's how "helping" connects to everything else we're doing in our life. Whether it's part of our job or not, the mission we're all on is one that involves creating as much value for as many people and organizations as we can. Yes, in the corporate sense, the measure of value creation is usually revenue, but in a broader sense, value can mean so many things—community, opportunities, emotional support.

What could possibly get in the way of spending fifteen minutes adding value to my friend's son, the friend who could hire him, the organization that could benefit from his work—and me, because now both of those people, and that company, are grateful and might think of me if there's an opportunity that would be beneficial on my end? The reason I can connect so many dots and create so many win-wins is because the more you live this way, the more people you know, and the larger the field from which you can make connections—for others or, if needed, for yourself. At its most basic level, it's just supply and demand. How do you help people come together in accretive ways that otherwise would not have happened? This is precisely how helping others helps us more.

HOW CAN YOU GIVE?

You can probably tell by now that we're getting to our next exercise. But first, a question: If giving makes sense, as I know it does, why don't we all give more? It's because even if we want to give, we perceive helping others as difficult to do in terms of time, effort, and direction—*How can I possibly give? It's hard, I'm busy, and I don't know where to start.*

Exercise 4.1

The heavier something is to lift, the less inclined we are to lift it. In the SEALs I used to joke when it was time to hit the gym, "I'd lift weights more often if they weren't so damn heavy." So how do we make giving lighter? How can we make giving something we are going to *actually* do, not just out of obligation but out of joy?

A big part of it is thinking about what kinds of help fit you best. Help doesn't necessarily mean going to the food bank, though it absolutely could. Step all the way back and ask: What are you good at? Is there any arena where you are the best in the world? The best in your community? Even the best in your house? On top of that, what do you enjoy doing? If you had endless time and energy, and we can even add that if budget wasn't an issue, how would you want to spend your time?

Make a list—eight, ten, fifteen things, anything that comes to mind. We are unconstrained at this point by how any of these activities might relate to giving or helping. Look at the list. Who can you share these joys with, who might really benefit? All the way back when I worked at Newport Creamery, I helped Bob the dishwasher be more efficient by showing him how I would load the dishwasher. I am really, really good at loading dishwashers. I think it's a SEAL thing. I can see how to fit everything efficiently, no problem. And I was happy to do it. All of us have things we know and can share. Who needs to know what you know—kids, adults, seniors—and can gain value from it? What can you do to make someone else's life easier? In what form can you do it?

A lot of people don't realize that giving can exist far outside of existing structures. I would obviously never discourage anyone from giving blood at a blood drive or running a race to raise money for one cause or another—but that's just the tip of the iceberg, and you do not need to be part of a larger organization in order to give. As I said earlier, one of the things Fred Kacher encouraged me to think about for the White House Fellows application essays was how I was already impacting the world. Military people struggle with this question—not because the work of being in the military doesn't impact the world enormously as it is, but because they think they need an answer beyond the job itself.

The military life is so regimented and very few people in the military out in the world on deployment come home and then go out to do organized volunteer work—bringing groceries to the elderly, etc. It just isn't what happens. Getting involved is hard when you're away from home for months out of the year. You're savoring time with family. You have no energy to do pretty much anything else. So it's hard to package it up sometimes in an application essay and make people realize that the service is their volunteerism and they simply converged volunteerism and their profession. They made their mission their job. Which is a good thing, in my mind, and not something to apologize for. Servicemen and women are as Mission Driven as people get, working on exactly the issues that move them and relate back to their *who*.

The exercise here is to find ways to live a life of service doing things you want to do anyway, and serve however you are most equipped to serve. I look at my friend Sara Wilkinson as the perfect example. Sara's husband, Chad, was one of my SEAL teammates and a close friend. While he technically reported to me, I, in fact, looked up to him because of the SEAL he was and the man he was. Tragically, Chad died by suicide in 2018 after twenty-one years of distinguished service. Sara, as anyone would be, was unsurprisingly in a dark and challenging place after that—but she knew, for Chad and for their family if not for herself, that she needed to find a way to move forward. Sara started a foundation in honor of Chad to support research for PTSD and raise awareness about suicide. Through my 1162 Foundation, I was able to help the Wilkinson family by paying off Sara's mortgage—which I knew would give her the freedom to pay it forward and touch the lives of so many others who need help. She is using the skills she has and the purpose she feels, doing her best to find her mission even in the face of terrible tragedy. Sara is making a hugely positive impact on the world and is as Mission Driven as can be. (Check out @sarawilkinson7 on Instagram!)

We are not all Sara Wilkinson. We cannot all do what she does, nor do we need to. We can be ourselves and still serve in worthwhile and unique ways.

WHEN IT'S TOO HARD

When we're overwhelmed, giving can feel like one more item on the to-do list. It can feel way too hard. But I would argue that when it feels too hard is exactly when you have to give more. You might have picked up this book thinking you need to invest more in yourself and don't have the time and energy to help others. It takes some self-awareness to acknowledge that you could be doing better at giving, and so I applaud you for that. But the fact that you're struggling might mean that you need to reframe how you're approaching each day and orient yourself a little differently.

Life is long, and of course there are times you will have more capacity to help and times you will have less capacity to help. But it's the times when you have less capacity that helping is so important, because it brings people and goodness into your life, and fills you with new appreciation for your fellow human beings. It comes back to my grandfather's advice about looking for someone having an even harder day when you're struggling. And back to Sara Wilkinson's story: No one would have blamed her for saying it was too hard to give. But giving is what lifted her up.

I can't finish this section without sharing the story of the truck driver who delivered a few thousand copies of *Never Enough* to my storage shed. He was the kind of guy who had a contagiously positive attitude while he went the extra mile, carrying things farther and helping more than he had to. I shared with him what he was helping with—the mission of my work, and the mission he was now a part of because his delivery was critically important. I explained that the proceeds were helping to pay off mortgages for Gold Star widows, to make the job more personal for him, more rewarding. When we were done offloading the truck, I thanked him profusely, and handed him a $100 tip. He took it and, without missing a beat, looked me straight in the eyes, handed it back to me, and softly said he wanted to be an even bigger part of the mission. He asked me to donate it to one of the great women who had sacrificed so much for this country. He said the whole reason he has a job and gets to live in America is because of these women and their families. I was speechless. I don't know why, but my throat started to close up. He made me proud to be an American. When you meet someone like that truck driver, who recognizes the sacrifice that my friends have made, you can't help but feel proud that we have citizens and patriots who give so much when they themselves also need. I was about to hand the money back and tell him I would make an equivalent donation in his name, but I realized donating the money had meaning for him, and I didn't want to deprive him of the opportunity to give. I will never forget him, and the reward I got that day was worth far greater than $100.

GIVING PAYS OFF IN THE END

I keep insisting that giving will pay off in the long run. That's not to minimize the short-term benefits. Visiting wounded warriors when I was in the SEALs was ostensibly for their benefit, but I always left those visits profoundly moved, inspired, and energized to be and do more. During my White House Fellow year, I brought my class-mates to the funeral of a SEAL teammate, Josh Harris, at Arlington National Cemetery. Josh was a rare renaissance SEAL who could paint, write poetry, take awesome pictures, and be the first SEAL on target, always knowing when, where, and how to be elite. To witness the somber yet beautiful community come together to cel-ebrate a hero's life, it was an hour of their time I hoped they would never forget (the same way John Connors's memorial service had an impact on me). I recently visited one of my friends who joined us that day. He just went through a bout with colon cancer. He told me that he thought back many times to that funeral, and while he knew his funeral wouldn't be at Arlington, he felt secure in the knowledge that he had friends and people he knew would show up and celebrate him. He told me he had often used our trip as a touchstone—what did he want *his* funeral to look like? More than fifteen years later, going to Arlington stayed with him, and probably others, and helped him think meaningfully about his own mortality. Was the trip to Arlington a gift? I think it was, even if it didn't necessarily feel like it at the time.

Giving pays off because a world in which we all are oriented toward giving is a better world. Individually, it pays off because if you make yourself worthy of being invested in, people will invest in you. Helpers recognize those same impulses in others; they understand who has the same orientation to give back and who does not. Giving also leads to more and more giving. You start out doing it because it's the right thing, and once you recognize that helping yields a great return, you keep on doing it. I think of it like planting seeds. You can throw half a bag of seeds on the lawn, and only a couple hundred will grow and turn into grass—but you don't get the full lawn unless you throw out a million seeds. And then of course the seeds that do grow will multiply and create more grass year after year.

I want to end this chapter with one final point: *It does not diminish the service you provide if you act strategically.* It does not make you a craven individual if you give in ways that you imagine might lead to opportunities in the future. The giving still counts, and it's important to realize that. Helping my friend's son get an internship still counts, even if as I make those phone calls, I use them as opportunities to remind the people I'm calling that I exist, and that I am always here to help them. It still counts if I use it as a chance to network an introduction to someone I might have never otherwise had a chance to meet.

It is perfectly okay and, in fact, entirely reasonable to invest in the kinds of giving activities that are more likely to come back to you in positive ways. My friend John Whitehead was a perfect example. John was a junior Naval officer on June 6, 1944, who drove infantry into Normandy, wave after wave. Later, he was chairman of Goldman Sachs, United States Deputy Secretary of State in the Reagan administration, and a recipient of the Presidential Citizens Medal. In his late eighties, he ran the commission that oversaw the reconstruction of Manhattan after 9/11, and did more charitable work than you could recount in an entire volume. He used to say, "Do something retail every day." By that, he meant touch someone and do something real—affect their life.

Where it crosses the line, perhaps, is in the genesis of the intention. People can tell the difference between giving so you can get—the wrong orientation—and what I'm saying, where you can choose how to give in ways more likely to be synergistic with the rest of your life. Over the last decade-plus, I've had a lot of what people might think of as extracurricular activities: my work with the National Medal of Honor Museum, The 1162 Foundation, writing two books. It does not diminish their value to acknowledge they have served me in my "day job." Giving doesn't have to be a separate endeavor. It can all work together.

This book is about realism, not fantasy. I'm not going to pretend that if you donate a kidney to a stranger—a true sacrifice that a small number of awesome people make every year, an act to be applauded—it will turn into the job opportunity of a lifetime. But I will say that if you do the right things, they add up. The world is not zero-sum. Giving is about making the pie bigger—others get, and you can get more as well. Gaining from giving doesn't mean someone else is losing. There are not a limited number of opportunities in the world. I am writing this book to help people, but it is no secret that its success will also give me a platform to do even more. That is a good thing, not an idea to run from.

It is a *wonderful* thing when giving pays off, because the more it pays off, the bigger your life becomes, and the more you are able to give. Baked into the journey upward on your mission is the promise that every time you have more opportunities, more knowledge, or more money, you can do more good. If you have a larger plat-form, you can help more people. Extending yourself to help others opens doors that may not have otherwise opened, and the positive feedback cycle that results is nothing to be ashamed of. Success is an unfettered good as long as you use it as a force for even more good. I think about my friend Nick Mehta, the CEO of Gainsight, a tech-nology company built around customer success. His platform helps companies measure whether they are successfully serving their cus-tomers. You can't understand the success of your business, after all, until you understand its impact on the people you are trying to help. In building this product, he has created significant success for him-self, his investors, and all of his employees—while at the same time helping end users because they're the ones who benefit from compa-nies better understanding their needs. Does it diminish the impact on customers if his business makes a profit? Not at all—and those end customers being well served would hopefully agree.

We are almost finished with "The Long Game"—one last idea to go. The next chapter is about what I call the meta-plan. Just like we build meta-skills, we can deploy them along a meta-plan, the path toward achieving our mission that we know is always changing and will always change. We cannot architect a direct line to our goal, but what we must do is figure out the best way to get there. Plans will always change, but as long as we keep that in mind, we can navigate even the toughest storms that threaten to throw us off course.

CHAPTER FIVE

Plans Will Always Change

Chris Cassidy is one of my closest friends and my "swim buddy" from SEAL training. He's a standout former SEAL who then became a NASA astronaut and the subject of the Disney+ documentary series *Among the Stars*. When we were shivering uncontrollably in frigid water during SEAL training, Chris never imagined that a couple of decades later he'd be flying through space (and, in fact, he sent me a photo of *Never Enough* in the International Space Station, which I posted on Instagram @thisis.mikehayes—the only commercial book ever, as far as I know, to be pictured in space!). "Despite all your best preparation and plans," Chris has said, "as soon as you step off the helicopter, as soon as you step into the mission, it's about to change."

We bonded in the water. One hundred and twenty of us started in BUD/S class 192 in 1993, and we were told at the very start to swim half a mile—thirty laps—in the pool as fast as we could. They needed to assign swim buddies for the training going forward, and wanted to pair people who swam at roughly the same speed because we had to stay within six feet of our swim buddy at all times in the ocean. We were the first and second who finished, and thus assigned as Swim Pair 1. With our class of 120 whittled down to 19 by the end, everyone else changed buddies at some point...but not us. We were there from beginning to end and did everything together. From BUD/S training we went to six more months of advanced training; there were no more ocean swims to pair up for, but we were roommates and dive buddies through all of it.

Together, we dove the sometimes surprisingly cold and lonely waters off Puerto Rico wearing 100% oxygen Dräger rebreather rigs, staying within a few feet of each other, fifteen to twenty feet under the surface of the water during the dark of night. It was pitch black and we had to navigate complicated patterns without surfacing, taking into consideration the ocean currents, to find small ships sometimes parked on piers miles away from our starting point. This was to simulate planting mines underneath the water without being detected and leaving no trace. Most people don't realize this, but 100% oxygen starts to become toxic in the body at twenty feet of depth and physiologically one of the first symptoms can be irritability. Chris and I to this day don't remember once being irritable, but we sure did see other dive pairs yelling at each other—which of course as twenty-two-year-olds, we did what any good young SEAL would do: laugh at and make fun of them (humor can often help in hard situations).

Chris and I landed on different SEAL Teams but our lives intersected again and again and our service to others is borne from our own hard moments. All of it made us personally and collectively better prepared to help others. Chris helped me with my application to become the SEALs first "Pol-Mil scholar" (Politico-Military) and with my subsequent graduate school applications, giving hard and helpful feedback that made the applications better, and later I helped review his essays for NASA's astronaut program. Our careers have been built on a simple principle: We're better together.

He was picked by NASA in 2004—out of thousands who apply—and ended up spending 377 days in space, doing ten space walks, a total of 54 hours outside the shuttle, among the most of any astronaut ever. Chris was unflappable as a SEAL, calm and collected under pressure, and I have no doubt that is what made him a success in space as well. Nothing throws him. Nothing flusters him. I look up to him immensely.

Chris's career—which has now taken him to the role of CEO of the National Medal of Honor Museum Foundation after retiring from the Navy and from NASA—has been all about change—jumping from hard setting to hard setting, without knowing for sure what would be next. But leaps like his are not unusual, especially when you keep mission at the center of what you do. Missions transcend career paths, which is why the people who are most Mission Driven end up having to perhaps navigate the most change in our lives and careers. We are always in search of what will get us closer to our *who* and so it is inevitable that we will have to shift.

Why is change such a constant in the lives of Mission Driven individuals?

On one level, career plans can simply change—over time, or in an instant. Opportunities may emerge, people may see things in us that we don't yet see in ourselves, businesses may close, and organizations may evolve in ways that do or don't match our missions. We need to feel confident making leaps and letting the world influence us rather than remaining stuck in situations that may no longer be ideal.

On another level, *we* change over time. Perhaps you are a person who has always wanted to be a doctor, and now you're a doctor. Why do you still need to worry about change? What if something happens to you and you can't be a doctor anymore? What if your wants or needs change and you haven't given yourself the space to realize it? Things outside of work may also change. As you ask how you're impacting the world, you may find you want to make shifts in terms of family, non-profit work, hobbies, areas of growth outside your career, or areas of growth deeper within your career. You need to be constantly checking in with yourself to make sure the things you assume are never going to change about yourself and your life *actually haven't changed.*

Finally, society changes. Circumstances change; technology changes; economies struggle; crises threaten to upend everything we have worked for. Seismic shifts happen over the course of every life, personal and global and on every scale between the two. Trouble will always find you, in some form or another, at some point now or in the future, and you need to think ahead to not just how you will act but how you will *decide* how to act, and who you want to be when those shifts arise: the person who rises and thrives, like Chris Cassidy, or the person who falls apart?

How do you navigate all of this change and make sure you don't get thrown off course? Yes, you may have the meta-skills to carry you through as the details of any particular role change, but what about when the mission itself changes?

Success in these moments is about having a plan for when the plan is no longer the plan. We need a *meta-plan* that can guide us when we're lost at sea and trying to figure out how to find the *who* that is at risk of going missing. How did Chris Cassidy go from the SEALs and space to CEO of a museum? The story is that I called him and told him that I think I know his next mission. He wasn't thinking about the CEO role until I broached the idea and it has turned out to be a perfect fit. No one could have excelled in this role better than Chris. In some ways, I know him better than he knows himself—and he knows me better than I know me.

The museum is about as Mission Driven as possible. I was initially asked by my friend Dave McCormick (I should say Senator Dave McCormick—more about him soon) to give someone he knew some advice. At that point, Dave's friend was thinking about building a small, local tribute to Medal of Honor recipients in South Carolina, to celebrate the brave American heroes awarded the nation's highest military decoration. It was just an idea he was batting around, and I told him that I thought his idea was too small. I immediately had a vision—this could be a national treasure, not just in brick and mortar, but with technology that could reach every American and truly inspire our country. We could not just tell the moving stories of the heroic medal recipients but build a testament to the values represented by the Medal of Honor: integrity, character, sacrifice, the willingness to fight for what you believe in, and of course, *mission*. No matter who you are and what you believe, it seems impossible to disagree with what the Medal of Honor stands for. I saw the potential for a place where children and adults could be inspired to be leaders, to serve, be moved, and move others. I talk a lot in this book about helping others help others; that's exactly the mission of the museum.

Dave's friend understood my reframing and higher-level vision completely, and as we continued talking, I happened to mention that I had just come from a breakfast group—a group I'd been invited to join by John Whitehead, the extraordinary human being and mentor I mentioned in the previous chapter. John had been meeting with friends once a month for breakfast for decades; after I spoke at an event honoring John on his ninetieth birthday, he invited me to join the group. Sadly, John passed away a couple of years later, but in those years we knew each other, I learned so much from him about service and helping. When I mentioned John's name, Dave's friend froze and started to tear up. As it turned out, John Whitehead was one of his mentors, and he'd missed John tremendously since he'd passed away three years earlier. He said he could not help but think that in some way John was looking down on him, giving him wisdom through my voice.

Given that connection and the value he saw in the advice I was giving him, Dave's friend asked me to be the first board member for this new vision of what could be a truly impactful national museum. I told him I needed a day to think about it. It's easy to give advice from the sidelines but joining a board involves a whole different level of responsibility and commitment—and I could already tell from our conversation that the existing board for the local effort was a mess, and this idea needed to be so much bigger, so much more than the board was envisioning at that point. There was infinite potential.

I came back to him the next day and said that I would do it but only if I could fire everyone on the existing board and we could start from scratch, with him as the founding CEO and me as the founding board member. It was a big condition to set, but I'd thought hard about it and truly believed this was the best and only path to success. You have to trust your convictions—especially when you're looking to undertake something that could be such a significant contributor to your mission.

He laughed and said now he needed a night to think. He called me the next day and said he was in. I ended up re-envisioning the museum entirely and created a new board filled with visionaries who saw the same potential as I did. Two years later, after selecting a location for the museum, we brought on other remarkable board members, including the wonderful Charlotte Jones, a national treasure and the daughter of Dallas Cowboys' owner Jerry Jones, along with Thasunda Brown Duckett, the CEO of TIAA, Neil Liebman, the COO and co-owner of the Texas Rangers baseball team, former Secretary of State and ExxonMobil CEO Rex Tillerson, and many more. It was a seven-year journey from my initial vision and concept for the museum in June 2018 to raising $300 million with phenomenal teammates. We opened our doors in Arlington, Texas, in March 2025, with thirty-two of the sixty-one living Medal of Honor recipients on hand along with NBC's Savannah Guthrie, country music star Lee Greenwood singing "God Bless the USA," and many others. Chris Cassidy has been my partner and teammate since he came in to lead the effort as CEO in 2021. It couldn't be more meaningful for me to open the doors to such an incredible place with my swim buddy from SEAL training three decades earlier.

The museum is so much more than a storehouse for old military paraphernalia, or even a way to recognize and honor those who have received the Medal of Honor. Instead, it's a place to highlight and platform the values and the character that America stands for. People can benefit so much from learning the heroic stories of servicepeople who have fought and triumphed over evil. Their lessons can inspire third graders on the schoolyard to step in when they see someone bullied, give adults in the workplace the confidence to act when they see something unethical or illegal, or help people see how important it is to praise others' success publicly. In so many ways the mission of the National Medal of Honor Museum is the same as the mission of this book: to help ordinary people do extraordinary things.

The heroes celebrated in the museum achieved their *who* one way: through military service to our nation. That journey is, for some people, an easy mission to visualize. Other missions can feel less straightforward—not easier or harder to achieve, but more difficult to conceive of. This is where planning becomes so important. But it's about more than planning. As with Chris Cassidy's journey, planning doesn't even begin to describe it. The twists and turns of our life can feel unpredictable and, indeed, *are* unpredictable. If someone tells me they know where they're going to be in three, five, ten years, they're either lying or they're just wrong. We can't know. Change will knock aside even the best plans, almost as soon as we make them.

You need more than a plan. Which is where the meta-plan comes in.

THE META-PLAN

The meta-plan is the culmination of "The Long Game," and it is a big part of what makes someone truly Mission Driven. We are always evolving, as people and as professionals. We can never know when we happen to be at an inflection point; it is often only through hindsight that we recognize the moments when everything shifted. Unless we engineer those moments ourselves. Each and every day we get to wake up and choose to either continue the path we're on or find a new one. A job you don't plan to leave can suddenly become a job you no longer have—or a better opportunity might present itself tomorrow. If it does, you need to have a framework within which to consider it. Even if you don't see this moment as a moment for change, you always have to be open to the possibility, or you will potentially miss reaching your greatest potential.

In the business context it's easy to explain the need for a meta-plan. A friend of mine ran the technology department for a large consumer bank, with multiple lines of business. A data center went down and their banking app wasn't working—an app that served tens of millions of people every day. It was, for this business, a game-changing crisis. The company had a hundred playbooks, but the specific problem with this data center was the 101st problem on the list. They simply hadn't anticipated it.

So what happened? Before they could solve the problem—and get back to business—they had to figure out *how* to solve it, who was in charge, what to communicate externally and internally, and in what order to proceed. They did fix the issue, but it wasn't without pain and it took longer than it should have. The company was exceptionally prepared for the hundred things they thought might go wrong, but for this one they were scrambling, and both the outcome and the path to the outcome were suboptimal—and certainly ate up resources that might have otherwise been deployed elsewhere.

What might they have done? A meta-plan could have told them to first figure out the most important outcome. The most important outcome is not going to be the same in every situation. This is a simplified example, for sure—every organization in today's world has a plan for what to do when a data center goes down—but the thinking process is still instructive. Sure, in this case you want to get the data center back up and running. But that's not really the outcome you need. The data center is important only as far as it makes it possible for the app to work. If you use all of your energy on fixing the data center, you might miss that there are alternative ways to fix the app—more quickly—without the data center.

The most important outcome here was getting the app running—but that wasn't even necessarily going to be the most important outcome in every scenario. Suppose the data center was on fire. Then the app would become a secondary concern, and the first thing you would need to do was make sure the people working there were safe and evacuated. In the meta-plan, someone would need to be in charge of figuring out what the number one goal was, no matter the situation. And if the app was going to be so important, in so many possible scenarios, the meta-plan would need to create redundancies so that one disaster—no matter what it was, the data center or otherwise—couldn't take it down. If all it took was one data center going down to mean a catastrophic loss for the business, no one was looking at the big picture and recognizing just how important data center redundancies and recovery really were. That's where the meta-plan comes in.

Most of the response to any crisis, after all, is about what's already in place pre-crisis—the people you train and how you train them, the culture of the business, the established flow of information. It's really hard to make choices about these things on the fly when you don't have a set of principles to turn to for guidance. It's hard to drive everyone in a company to immediately understand where to focus their attention if you don't set that up in advance. That is the meta-plan. "Our customers come first, no matter what." With a guideline like that in place—a mission statement, really—regardless of what happens, you know what to do.

A meta-plan frees you from worrying about short-term impacts and assures you it's okay to keep the long run in mind. In the SEALs, we dealt with this all the time. In any crisis, we had to assume things would get worse. We couldn't just solve for the moment. We had to solve for all the moments that would reverberate down the line—keeping in mind what else might go wrong and the need to compete for resources. We didn't just look at each choice in a vacuum.

Consider someone in the services sector—an accountant, architect, property manager, or plumber—being approached with too many projects to handle. Each project comes to her, and she has to make a binary decision: take it on, or turn it down. Most contractors have an uncertain stream of work. There is risk in turning anything down, but of course, there is also risk in taking on too much. The answer to any given project may be, "Yes, of course I can do it," but if you add up all the yeses, you have to know where to draw the line. That line depends on whether the meta-plan points you to maximizing income at the cost of anything else, or perhaps there are other priorities in life you want to keep space for. It's not that one choice is right or wrong, but if you don't know going into a meeting what you're trying to achieve, it makes it really hard to decide what to do.

All of this applies no less when there's a crisis in life rather than at work. The meta-plan tells you where your focus is. You may be juggling care for kids and aging parents—but have you thought about what you do when those responsibilities collide? Is a backup plan easier in one case than another? Are there people who can help, services and relationships already set up? What happens when your child is sick? How do you make the decision as to which parent stays home, if one of them staying home is, in fact, the plan?

Exercise 5.1

Before we get to making your own meta-plan, take a moment to think about where you're starting from. Take the following hypotheticals and consider how you would respond:

- Your boss asks you to move to China for two years to start a new office. How do you make the decision whether or not to go?
- You get called about a new job opportunity. How do you decide if it's the right fit for you, or whether there are other, better options out there?
- A family member is having a crisis and asks you to drop everything and come help them for an indefinite amount of time. How would you respond?

There are no right or wrong answers, but thought exercises like this are valuable because they let you know how you approach big decisions right now. Do you have an organized system for analyzing what you should do? What questions do you need to ask? What is most important in making these choices? The struggle to even know where to begin the analysis is why the meta-plan we'll craft very soon can be so critical, and it highlights the point that it's really not about the decisions themselves but the process to make them, and the logic behind the thinking. You may never need to make the same decision twice, but the way you make the decision is what gets reapplied again and again and enables you to compound knowledge and wisdom over the course of your whole life.

META-PLANNING IN ACTION

As I've said before, people look at my career and think I've jumped from sector to sector with little to tie the experiences together. But they don't understand that every move has been driven by a meta-plan sitting on top of the decision-making process. When faced with a potential opportunity, I ask myself: Will this opportunity increase my ability to have the greatest possible impact? The industry is secondary—but I understand that only because I've taken the time to drill down on what my mission really is, and how I'm going to achieve my *who*.

With the right overarching priorities in mind, decision making becomes far easier. If you tell me that your meta-plan involves the search for ultimate financial freedom, that is going to yield different answers at almost every turn than if you tell me you're looking for day-to-day security. If you tell me you want to be on the path to becoming a CEO, that will yield different answers than if you tell me you don't want to relocate or travel much. Without a meta-plan in the background, if you get a job offer from, say, a high-risk, high-reward startup, it's hard to know where to begin to analyze the choice.

Exercise 5.2

We're going to build your meta-plan.

You start, once more, with your *who*. Who do you want to be? What is your mission? If that's the desired outcome, how do you get there? The meta-plan is about making your *who* actionable. If you are someone who wants to make a difference in the world by, say, running for office, then your meta-plan might involve a series of principles that emerge when you think about how to reach that goal. In any given scenario, your priority is going to be to preserve the possibility of being elected. So you want to avoid personal scandal, connect with as many individuals as possible, demonstrate leadership, and pay attention to the optics of any decision you make. Short-term outcomes are less important than long-term outcomes for you, and financial outcomes lag far behind.

At the top of a piece of a paper, write your success definition from Exercise 2.3. And then think about the questions that would lead you closer or farther away from each element of success. Suppose, just as an example, on the personal front, your success definition involves being present for your children, making sure they get the best-quality education, reaching financial security, and optimizing your physical health and well-being. Then you might come up with the following questions:

- Will this give me more time with my children?
- Will it affect my children's education?

- Will this make it more likely I reach financial success?
- Will it help me in terms of my physical health?

These become the top-line principles of your meta-plan. There may be questions you want to nest underneath: more granular questions in terms of guiding your decisions. For instance, take the first question:

- Will this give me more time with my children?
    * Is the answer different short-term vs. long-term?
    * Will the quality of the time be impacted by my choice?
      ...And so forth.

After you've written the questions, you need to come up with contingency options to cover when your decision may not be perfect across all dimensions. Perhaps you decide to take a new job that will provide more flexibility (more time with your kids) but force a move to a worse school district (a negative for their education). Using this same simplified example, you might plan out something like the following:

- If a decision will not be a plus for my children's education:
    * Do we have enrichment programs in mind, to use as needed?
    * Have we identified tutors for supplementation?
    * Could we homeschool? How might that work in practice?

For an organization, or in a business context, the thinking is very much the same. What are the big-picture questions, and then what are the more granular questions that fall beneath?

Keep in mind this is not a one-time exercise. We need to constantly check back and make sure the same factors that were at the top of the list are still the ones that belong there. If not, a crisis will hit and you'll be moving in the right direction to reach the wrong outcome. Every time a situation plays out, you should go back to the meta-plan and ask if the choice was right. Have you learned any new information about the world that can make your decision even better next time? The only way we'll make better decisions in the future is if we incorporate knowledge of what did and didn't work in the past.

THE POWER OF THE META-PLAN

The meta-plan provides at least five benefits.

First, it can take the pressure off. Too often, we try to over-engineer our lives because we think we know the best path to a particular destination. But if we try to control everything too tightly—without making space for the unexpected—we will be disappointed. The existence of a meta-plan acknowledges we don't always have control and there will always be curveballs. We can't hold ourselves to the (impossible) expectation that we can plan for everything, and that we always know what's to come. Instead, a meta-plan helps us embrace the idea that the unexpected will come and gives us a framework of questions so we can trust we will be ready.

Second, it can optimize decision making. Making decisions in stressful moments is hard. The more you can pre-make those decisions, or at least pre-craft the guidelines with which to make them, the better your decisions will be. If we have a rubric already in place, against which to evaluate choices, we can be intentional even when we have little time or distracted focus.

Third, it creates the space for external validation. Having others weigh in on a decision is important to increase confidence. You never want to be making decisions in a bubble, without other people's perspectives potentially catching holes in your thinking. In an emergency, there may not be time to figure out who to talk to. But a meta-plan can be vetted in advance, as well as identify the right people to bring in when those emergencies strike. It's a lot easier to tell someone in advance that they're on call in case the data center goes down rather than trying to figure out in the moment who should be in charge and bringing them up to speed.

Fourth, creating the meta-plan helps you figure out your own priorities and whether you're looking to maximize short-term or long-term outcomes. The act of sitting down and thinking through the possible directions you might want to head, depending on the situation, forces you to confront the reality that you can't always achieve everything you want. If the Swedish travel company had worked on a meta-plan in advance, they would have grappled with deciding whether short-term profit was the most important goal, or if thinking about the long-term, their reputation, and customer satisfaction was going to help them better achieve their desired end state. The more thinking you can do in times of stability, the easier it is to prioritize and make principled decisions when crises strike.

Finally, making a meta-plan helps you understand the full range of options and resources you have. In the moment, it's hard to remember there is a redundant data center waiting on standby, or you have an extra ship in the ocean ready to look for lost travelers.

Or if you don't have those things, making the meta-plan can help you realize those might be things to invest in now, before the situation demands it. If you decide in advance that your number one priority is going to be keeping your mobile app up and running, making a meta-plan will help you realize you need a backup, and maybe a backup for the backup, and you need them in different locations, with people ready to act immediately if the main center goes down. You can't put those contingency plans in place in an instant, so having the meta-plan ready beforehand is necessary to avoid the worst-case scenarios. The same goes for the personal example above. If you consider possibilities in advance, you may realize home-schooling would be a reasonable choice for your family, if you had to move to an area without an ideal school. You can get that option ready in advance, pre-selecting a curriculum, etc.

There was an old saying that one of the early commanders of Special Operations Command (SOCOM), General Wayne Downing, used to repeat: "Special Operations forces can't be built overnight." Special Operations forces are the contingency units for crises: You will need them, but you never know quite when or quite why until the crisis happens. And since you can't build them overnight, the point was that you need to always be funding, building, and improving Special Operations forces so they are ready when the need strikes.

SHINING A LIGHT

The meta-plan is the flashlight that gets us through the darkness, when what's next isn't clear and all we can do is our best. I started this chapter with Chris Cassidy and I'm going to end it with another hero, SEAL Command Master Chief Britt Slabinski. "Slab" was on the other end of one of the first two calls I made when we started building the Medal of Honor Museum, but his story really starts nearly two decades earlier. Back in 2002, Slab, with more than a decade of SEAL experience at the time, thought he was prepared for anything. And then he ended up on snow-covered Takur Ghar Mountain in the remote hills of Afghanistan six months post-9/11 on a mission to survey the area and gather information about where the enemy was hiding. He and his team were told by military intelligence that no one was on top of the mountain. That intelligence was wrong. Immediately upon landing in their helicopter and lowering the ramp, they were hit with grenades and withering machine gun fire. The helicopter's electricity was taken out by a rocket, but they knew they had to evacuate just as soon as they'd arrived. Britt's teammate (and my friend) Neil Roberts was thrown out. He fell ten feet from the helicopter ramp onto the ground shortly after the rocket's impact. The pilot and crew, dealing with failing hydraulics and engine power, without weapons and navigation aides, managed to put the aircraft down some distance away from Neil in enemy territory.

Britt's meta-plan left no doubt: They were going back for Neil, despite the risk. They landed again and found themselves in a gunfight, right away. Teammates were down, some wounded, some dead. It was the kind of worst-nightmare operation that you train for but hope to never experience. Britt and his teammates fought the enemy, called in close air support, treated the wounded, and dragged them through the mountainous terrain and frigid conditions to a defendable location until they themselves could be rescued. They ended up spending twenty-three hours on the mountain, fourteen of them in direct combat. For his bravery in going back for Neil, who ultimately could not be saved, Britt was awarded the Medal of Honor. "His dedication, disregard for his own personal safety, and tactical leadership make Master Chief Slabinski unquestionably deserving of this honor," the official citation reads.

Britt spent years after that day not quite sure about his mission, not certain where his meta-plan should take him next. He has been open in talking about his struggles; as he says, "everyone on that mountain left a piece of themselves up there," and I'd make the case that pretty much everyone who has ever seen combat like that lives at times with a deep, deep sadness inside ourselves that arises whenever we're reminded of our teammates who are no longer with us. The question is how to try and overcome that and work to channel it toward something great. Not everyone can, and I pass no judgment on those who can't get past the struggle. I know just how hard it is. But Slab is committed to using the Medal of Honor to influence others and lift them up—and that's why he was one of the first calls I made when building the museum.

Slab joined me as a founding board member and has been a huge part of shaping the vision and strategy for the museum—and then working to make it happen. His life is all about spreading the inspiring stories of the Medal of Honor: The living Medal of Honor recipients have shown their faith in his work by electing him president of the Medal of Honor Society, to represent them and carry their legacy forward. Britt could have let torment bring him down, but he has used it as rocket fuel to figure out how to move forward and make an impact. His meta-plan—*make a difference, in the best way I know how*—has driven him.

But it doesn't need to take a gunfight on a snowy, enemy-covered mountain to make you step back and think about where you fit into the world. It is a superpower to look at your life with distance and wisdom. Making your own meta-plan is part of how you train yourself to see things from multiple angles. To gather different sources of information. To make better decisions. This all holds true no matter who you are, where you work, and what you feel your ultimate purpose on this planet is.

As we finish up this first half of the book and move to "The Short Game," this is where we stand: Who are you? Are you aiming for the right things? Do you have the plans in place to make the difference you want to make, and to leave the world a better place than when you arrived?

By now, you should have more clarity on the big picture. You should have a better sense of where you want to go and how you can make the important decisions along the way.

But what about the little ones? What about the next job, the next opportunity, the new thing you're going to do when you wake up tomorrow morning—that you've never done before?

Achieving your mission in the Long Game is all about the constant stream of decisions you make in the Short Game—and that's where we turn next.

THE SHORT GAME

CHAPTER SIX

Getting Comfortable Making Decisions

The first half of this book was about defining the mission: *Who do you want to be*, and what kind of life do you want to live? This half of the book is about putting that vision into action, year by year, week by week, and even moment by moment—driving yourself toward the mission you've just identified.

Where does that start? At every turn, we're forced to make decisions. Even when we think we're avoiding a decision—by staying put, by telling ourselves that we'll decide soon, by continuing to pursue the status quo—that is a decision in itself. The things we choose not to decide are equally if not more important than the active choices we make.

This is why it's critical to get as comfortable as we can when making decisions and, in doing so, make the most of the time and energy we have. No more leaning out and away. No more avoiding conflict. As with anything in life, we can never ignore the limits imposed by time and energy: There is an opportunity cost to every decision we make. But outcomes aren't always predictable. We can't know what we've missed when we invest energy in one direction rather than another; all we can do is make the best choice at the time. So how do you make those choices without paralysis and without regret?

We can learn from big decisions made by the most successful among us.

My great friend Dave McCormick went from the US Army's 82nd Airborne Division to earning a PhD from Princeton, then to business, to government (as Under Secretary of the Treasury for International Affairs under President George W. Bush—where I met him when I was at the National Security Council) then back to the private sector (where I joined him at Bridgewater), and now back into government as a recently elected US senator from Pennsylvania. No one has navigated between the public and private sectors better and his is an impressive journey that, if nothing else, has been filled with decisions. Knowing when to jump and where to jump is critical.

Billionaire software entrepreneur Marc Benioff, cofounder of Salesforce, provides an example of someone who made a big choice—a surprising one, to many. He was earning millions of dollars a year as an executive at Oracle but reached a point where he didn't feel fulfilled. His day-to-day wasn't enough. What did he do? He took a three-month sabbatical, went to India, and came back with newfound motivation, leaving two years later to launch his own business. Did he know that was how it would play out? Of course not, but he knew he needed something different in his life and he wasn't afraid to pursue it. How many people have built multibillion-dollar businesses by stepping away and clearing space to think and create? What can we learn from Marc's choice? What can we learn from Dave's choices?

What can we learn from my friend Ron Clark, whose late wife, Dr. Shannon Kula Clark, I celebrated in chapter 1? Ron and I both served in Iraq and also in the White House, advising the president on everything from protecting the United States against terrorist plots to preventing international conflicts from becoming all-out wars. Ron has also served as an assistant professor at the University of Virginia, the CEO of a private sector risk management firm, and a private equity adviser. How does he decide what is worth his energy and time, and what choices to make when opportunities come his way?

From all three of these impressive individuals, we can glean one larger truth: Big decisions, big shifts, big moves in your life and career sometimes lead to greatness. Not always, of course, but we can't be afraid to make big leaps, and we can't remain tentative when more is possible. Sometimes the decision is to stand still, but that's still a choice. And we have to be comfortable deciding, one way or the other, confidently, securely, and often quickly.

HOW DO WE MAKE DECISIONS?

At the most basic level, we can look to our meta-plan when faced with a choice or an opportunity. Does this fit? Does it get us closer to our goals in an efficient way? The answer isn't always obvious. Take a very granular example. Figuring out, say, whether to spend the next three hours making an incremental improvement in a PowerPoint deck or taking a walk with a new friend who might enrich your life in a variety of unpredictable ways is a choice about marginal impact. What do I mean by marginal impact? Marginal impact is simply the additional benefit that one choice might generate over another. It might be that this PowerPoint deck is going to mean the difference between a million-dollar deal or losing your job, in which case the impact is gigantic. It might also be that finding a missing comma is not going to change anyone's life, while your friend might be coming to you with an awesome opportunity.

There is no always-right or always-wrong answer here. It's about the specifics of the situation and making the decision with intention. It's probably more fun to take the walk with a friend, and so maybe that's the right decision, most of the time. But there are going to be Power-Points that do matter, and your walk might be able to be rescheduled.

The reality is that we can only know the outcome of the path traveled. We live one life—and that's hard. So many of us carry around regret over decisions we didn't make, or bad choices we did. My first response is it's okay not to be perfect. We all make mistakes. Reconciling our *who* and an error in life—big or small—doesn't degrade who we want to be and who we still can be. Maybe I shouldn't have left the SEALs when I did. I love my life and am grateful for every piece of it, but maybe if I'd stayed for another two years, I would have ended up on a far different path, and maybe it would have been a path even more impactful than the one I'm on.

All we can do is make the best choices at the time with the information we have. Making sure those decisions are active ones— looking at every possibility, leaving no stone unturned—lets you look back and say you did as well as you could. No regrets! (And remember, the outcomes of the path traveled sometimes take years to materialize. What feels like a mistake right now may very well feel like the best choice you could have made five years from now. We don't know.)

NOT JUST ABOUT DOING THE HARD THING

Approaching the moment-to-moment across our entire lives is a game of constant calibration. Which doesn't mean you can never relax and veg out on the couch for an evening. It may very well be that a night off—a few hours or even a week or a month of rest—will reinvigorate you and make the next day, week, or month far more efficient than it would have been otherwise.

In that spirit, I don't want anyone to take away from this book that being Mission Driven means that you can never rest. Although in *Never Enough* I wrote about choosing the hard path, and I've written in this book about making hard choices as well—I chose Bridgewater because it was the hard path, as just one example—I would say that it is always—always—up to you, and my inclination to take the hard path may not be yours.

I think about Rick Smethers, one of my early SEAL Team commanding officers. On his last day in the unit, Rick pulled me aside and said, "Mike, you have a limitless future but I can see you will get pulled in many directions. Our community tends to tell rising high-potential officers like you that you need to spend time not just in the SEAL Teams but with other commands that will give you professional diversity. None of those are as fun as the SEAL Teams. Those other opportunities will always be there, but you live one life. Take my advice: *Always take the good job now.*"

Rick assured me that I will perform better and be happier if I pick the job I am really going to enjoy, and that's the key—better, happier performance—to getting ahead, not ticking off boxes. I kept Rick's advice in the back of my mind even as I was trying to push myself to do the hardest thing at every turn. I realized that all I wanted to do was be a SEAL at a SEAL Team, and so I did as much of that as any officer could. I never did a tour with our boat units or underwater submarines (even if it would have theoretically broadened my experience), choosing instead to serve and deploy with all four East Coast SEAL Teams (TWO, FOUR, EIGHT, and TEN) and going overseas at every leadership level. Thirteen of my twenty years as a SEAL were spent deployed with SEAL Teams. Doing hard things wasn't the only decision criteria. It came back to my meta-plan. There were more questions worth asking.

Along similar lines, when I was picked as the first SEAL for the Navy's Pol-Mil program and awarded a two-year scholarship to any grad school I could get into, some cautioned me against disappearing for two years at Harvard because when the screenings for promotion happened, I would be "out of sight and out of mind." I was unmoved: If getting a graduate education was going to diminish my chances of getting promoted, I would happily not promote and go find some other organization to contribute to instead. In that case, I don't know if Harvard was the hardest thing I could have done or just the one I wanted to do, but hard wasn't the only factor. It was merely one of them.

It's never about doing what's harder just because it's hard. It's about doing what will compound most in the future. In some instances, you do what's hard right now because it gives you skills or grows relationships that you can use to create more options in the future—but if that's not the case, and the easier road is also what opens up more for you going forward, then you may not want to do what's hard just because it's hard. There has to be a purpose to the challenge.

It is not always easy to operationalize the idea that *hard* is separate from *best* across the different facets of your life. Suppose, say, one of your goals is to find a partner and have a family. The hard work there is going on dates, which take up time and energy. Yes, there's speed dating, where you can have 20 three-minute conversations in an hour with a lot of awkward rotating, but that's not an *exponential* leap in the number of people you can meet, and those meetings are not necessarily going to be so useful, because they're short.

So what other life decisions can you make? You can tell everyone you know or meet that you are looking for someone—and then they may find themselves looking for a match for you as well. (And, of course, you want to be crisp and specific about what you're looking for, so that people can make the right introductions—but we'll get there in chapter 8.) In the past, people took out personal ads; now, of course, there are dating apps, which also increase the number of people who become aware of you, for better or worse. These activities are not harder than going on a lot of dates, and they may not be better—but my point is to think about everything you do through this lens. Consider all options and see which one seems most likely to accomplish the goal, whether it's the hardest activity or not.

DECISIONS AT YOUR GREATEST INFLECTION POINTS

We all understand that there are big inflection points in our lives. In the SEALs, every two to three years, you finished your job, and you had to choose something else. "What are you doing next?" was a constant question.

The answers were not always easy, because every role had its advantages but also its drawbacks. What I realized along the way was that being forced to regularly make those big decisions allows you to figure out what really matters to you and helps you hone your process. I want to walk you through my thinking at a couple of major transition points for me, so you understand what the decision-making process can look like, before we dive into the details and give you a concrete plan of action in the next chapter.

As a platoon commander in Kosovo, for instance, I wasn't allowed by my commanding officer to go home to see my daughter's birth during a clear break in the reconnaissance operations we were doing. Had I known this guy's views on this topic were so rigid—*no one can go home!*—maybe I would have chosen a different rotation for that time in my life. What it did help me do was clarify my priorities. The experience caused me to make the decision never to put my own men in the same position: Whenever possible, when I was in charge, I not only allowed but encouraged everyone on my team to go home to see their kids being born.

During that rotation, I screened positively for SEAL Team SIX with three other SEAL officers in the country. In a time before 9/11, SEAL Team SIX was where all the operations happened—and where just about every SEAL wanted to be. That same rigid commanding officer wouldn't let me come home from my deployment to Kosovo a few weeks early to start SEAL Team SIX's annual selection training. I was upset and made the (perhaps rash) decision to leave the SEALs and go to grad school (this was a few years before the Pol-Mil program was on my radar screen, and years before the decision I explained earlier, where I ultimately left the SEALs after being downgraded in my evaluation). As I was still finalizing the choice, this same commanding officer told me about a new program where a few SEAL officers would be chosen as "task unit commanders," in charge of two platoons, or twice the number of people I'd led in my previous role. He told me I had already been selected, if I wanted the role.

In my mind, this was not as good as SEAL Team SIX, so I did still feel a little bad about it. But I had to decide: Do I leave, a little bit out of spite because he didn't let me do what I wanted to do, or do I stay and still do something bigger and cooler than the role I'd just completed? I realized I had to put the SEAL Team SIX situation out of my head and make a rational choice between the two paths that were open to me. (And, in fact, there were more than just two paths, of course—I didn't have to choose either the Task Unit role or graduate school, but those were the two most obvious paths at the time.)

That time, as opposed to when I decided to leave years later in a similar feeling of frustration, I chose to stay. Why? Partly because I liked being a SEAL and serving the country, and partly because the task unit commander role, if I stopped comparing it to SEAL Team SIX, seemed like a worthwhile opportunity. I realized I could contribute—and also grow. Every role should satisfy those two requirements: It's not enough to merely contribute if you're not growing, and your growth is secondary if you're not able to contribute along the way. There used to be an old Communist joke: "They pretend to pay us, and we pretend to work." Here, I didn't want to merely get paid for working; I wanted there to be more to my life than that.

I also made the choice because I thought about the future. I could always go to grad school, but I would not get to be a SEAL leader again once I got off the track. I felt called to lead, and that my impact as a SEAL leader would be greater than my impact would be going to grad school at the time. So I made the decision and tried not to look back.

How might it have turned out if I went to grad school then, instead of a few years later? As I said, we can never know the impact of decisions we don't make—I did the best I could at the time. No regrets!

When I did end up going to grad school, the impetus was different. Post-9/11, I was overseas leading a SEAL Task Force in Germany, and we were supposed to go into Iraq through Turkey. But we ended up stuck in Germany because of international bureaucracy, and so I had a whole group of exceptional SEALs who didn't get to contribute to the war effort at that time. We were ready to serve, and we just...weren't able to. I realized at that point maybe I needed a new challenge. I felt like I had gotten really good at being a SEAL, but I wanted to do something more intellectual for a little while, to gain experience so I could do more, whether in the SEALs or outside in the world. I figured a great grad school experience would serve me well the rest of my life regardless. And I ended up bringing that back to the SEALs when I was finished, serving eight more years and seeing more combat than anyone should wish for.

When I finally did decide to leave, after the annual evaluation issue, I was in Afghanistan on my seventh deployment of six months or more away from my family. I was gone for ten months that time, and had reached the pinnacle of what a SEAL can do in combat. I was running not just a SEAL Team, but an entire 2000-person Special Operations Task Force and everything we were doing in southeastern Afghanistan, sleeping three hours a night. What it means to be a commanding officer is that the pace of your life is nonstop. You do not have a chance to breathe. The next step up was going to be far more of an administrative role, so even before the frustration about where I was ranked among my peers, I was already thinking about what I wanted to do next.

There is a piece of wisdom that circulates among military leaders, and it's about exactly this topic of making important decisions: Never make a career decision when you're on deployment. The emotions are just too heavy. And so I waited until I was home. I thought back to my White House days and realized that some people know the public sector, some people know the private sector, but very few know both—among them, a whole bunch of people I've already mentioned in this book, like Ron Clark and Dave McCormick. I saw that the most impactful people were the ones who not only knew both worlds but could connect the two in unexpected ways.

I was deployed until October 2012. I made the final decision to leave that December, and the Navy did me a solid and created a role for me with two other close friends, Rear Admiral Scott Moore and Medal of Honor recipient Britt Slabinski, so we could have administrative roles to transition from and time to figure out what was going to be next. I began to hustle—in ways I didn't realize at the time were the subject of the next chapter in this book. I had conversations to learn the landscape of what was possible and how to find a role where I would be learning as well as creating real impact. Those conversations—what I call Level 1 conversations, and you'll understand what those are in chapter 7—led me to a bunch of banks and investment firms, private equity, venture capital, and young businesses, until finally I made the decision to go to the world's largest hedge fund, Bridgewater.

I will talk in the next chapter about balancing substance and perception. This is a key distinction to make when you're thinking about your options. Whether a particular role is open to you is often about perception: Do others see you as capable of filling the job? But whether you are actually capable is about substance. Sometimes the two of them match, but often they don't. I knew that graduate school, for instance, would provide actual substance in the form of learning, but also create the perception that I was more than just a SEAL. I knew I needed to create that perception—as well as have substantive knowledge beyond the limited world I had seen professionally—and so grad school had been a relatively easy decision.

What I know now is I would have never been a White House Fellow without grad school. I didn't even know back then what the White House Fellows were, not until Professor Roger Porter, a former White House Fellow himself and adviser to three presidents, came to the Kennedy School, where I had just started my two-year graduate program, to talk about the White House Fellows. Everyone wants to be a White House Fellow when they first hear about it, but in listening to Professor Porter, I saw a plan—three more years at a SEAL Team as second in charge (or "executive officer") with a combat deployment after grad school, and then after that job, I knew I would be a White House Fellow. (Of course, there are thousands who apply and only fourteen are picked each year, but it was crystal clear to me walking out of the classroom that afternoon that it could and would happen.)

Even beyond grad school, being a White House Fellow—getting to work inside the government and learning from and being around leaders at the highest level—would surely give me both the substance and perception to be able to do almost anything I chose to.

That session with Roger Porter created the ultimate inflection point for me. And I got there because all along the way I was making intentional decisions designed to move me closer to my goal. I continued to do my very best to be the greatest SEAL I could be, leading in Iraq at the height of the war—after all, for as much thinking ahead as you might do, you can't forget that the only way to get anywhere is to do and be the absolute best at the job you have. But I did look multiple steps ahead to try to visualize the range of pathways.

If you had asked me thirty years ago what I'd be doing today, I'm sure the answer I would have given would be far from the reality of what my life now looks like. I didn't know anything about the corporate world when I was a twenty-something-year-old kid in the SEALs, and I certainly hadn't considered the idea that I'd ever start my own nonprofit or write a book, let alone two of them. I loved being a SEAL and didn't know where it was going to eventually take me—but I did know that I wanted it to take me somewhere. The way we get there, wherever it ends up being, is step by step, choice by choice.

EVERY MOMENT CAN BE AN INFLECTION POINT

This is a point I really want to emphasize. It is not just about the big moments that we know at the time are big moments. Every moment, once again, is a decision to either keep doing what you're doing or do something else. Every moment is a chance to repair a relationship, seek out something new, go deeper wherever you are, or switch gears to something entirely new. The email you decide, on the spur of the moment, to send to a friend could be the email that changes the rest of your life. Or it may just be an email. Until you send it, you will never know.

But saying that every moment can be an inflection point is different from saying that every moment *is* an inflection point. No one wants to be changing his life twelve times a day, and even using the mental energy to consider big change at every moment can be draining and unproductive.

Instead, we need a framework to make as much of the decision making as automatic as we can.

Exercise 6.1

Go all the way back to your *who*. At the top of a piece of paper, write out all the separate elements. This is an exercise we could have done in chapter 1, but I wanted to wait until you had done all the Long Game thinking before we tried to construct a path to your *who*. Remember, we've already looked at how your *who* translates into success, what others think about your *who*, what you're doing that you shouldn't be, how to get 1% better, how to help others, and how to evaluate decisions using a meta-plan.

Now, underneath each element of your *who*, list some concrete steps you could take in order to get yourself there. What do I mean? Suppose you want to be a person with greater ties to your community. Ask yourself, in practical terms: How would that happen? At the most impactful level, you could start a civic organization focused on bringing some type of change or benefit to your neighborhood. What kind?

Think of perhaps a dozen—we're brainstorming ideas here, not committing to a plan—and write them down. At a smaller level, you could invite someone to dinner, bring someone a pie, help your kids make a lemonade stand. Write those ideas down, too. Go through every element of the *who* you want to be and brainstorm a set of options to get closer, choices you have within your power to make.

This should be a pretty long list. Some of them are going to be more interesting than others, more impactful than others, and more realistic than others. Are there some you could take a step toward accomplishing today? This week? This month? There probably are, and each one will get you closer to becoming the person you want to be, and living the life you want to be living. Here in the Short Game, we are finally putting our big plans into action. Hold on to these ideas, think about which might be worth pursuing right now, and which might be worth building toward in the future.

LEARN FROM PAST DECISIONS

As we finish our deep dive into decision making: The final step in any decision-making process is evaluating the success of your decision, and if things didn't work out the way you hoped, figuring out where it went wrong. Sometimes things don't work out for reasons beyond our control—the world is unpredictable, people are unpredictable, and even the best decisions don't always yield good results. That doesn't mean the process wasn't good, but often there is reflection that can help us improve next time. Just like I learned (too late) that it was important to know if I'd have the flexibility to see my daughter being born, decisions that work out differently from how we might expect can help us clarify our priorities, sharpen our analysis, and do better next time. In the SEALs, we always ask what we could have done better regardless of whether any blame is ours to shoulder.

Even better than learning from our own mistakes is learning from the mistakes of others—and avoiding those mistakes ourselves. There are, of course, infinite mistakes we could learn from, but it is helpful in making our own decisions to understand what others did and why those choices did or didn't work out. This is part of why I wanted to explain my own choices in my career. You can ask yourself if you would have made the same choices or different ones. Would you have left the SEALs when I did? Would you have gone to grad school? Moved to the private sector?

But you have your own network of people in your life who have made decisions, successful and otherwise, and you can learn from them.

Exercise 6.2

Sit down with a friend or colleague—perhaps two or three of them—and ask them to walk you through the best and worst decisions they've ever made. How did they make them, and what can they teach you about your own decision making? Do you agree with their process and their reflection? Or do you feel differently?

Hearing about people's failures is often more useful than knowing their successes. I've learned a ton of great interview questions over the years and often use one I was asked in my White House Fellow interview: What's the most profound ethical dilemma you've ever faced...where you failed to do the right thing? Asking this question is how you see someone's struggles, where they may be weak or prone to error. Think about an ethical dilemma where you did the wrong thing. Does that help give you perspective on big decisions you might make in the future?

Maybe you don't want to admit you've "failed" in any ethical situation—but that's part of what I draw from someone's answer. Can you at least identify something meaningful in your life where you wish for the magical "do-over"? If not, that's frankly a big interview red flag for me.

In the next chapter, we move from decision making in general to one more specific type of decision that we all make multiple times in our life in a large sense—our career, our role, our job—and in a micro-sense every single day. How do we decide how we spend our time—professionally and otherwise—and make sure we are always Mission Driven?

CHAPTER SEVEN

Mission Driven in the Ways
We Spend Our Time

I exchanged emails recently with a Navy SEAL who reached out after hearing me give a talk. He wanted to know what he should do next in his career, and said he felt like he didn't even know how to begin thinking about life after the SEALs.

In some ways, his note was the inspiration for this entire book, because I was desperate to have something to hand him—some kind of actionable framework for making decisions like this. You've now spent six chapters thinking about *who* you want to be in the world, what success means, and the right way to think about decision making. Here is where the rubber meets the road: You want to find your next great opportunity; *what do you do?*

It's a conversation I've had hundreds of times. And while, for most people, it's about finding a job, I intentionally made the title of this chapter broader than that. Just like everyone's priorities are different, where we each find our mission is different as well. For me, my job is part of it—a big part of it—but to focus exclusively on my job misses the bigger picture. My mission is also present in my nonprofit work, my writing, my friends, and my family. So many people have "side hustles" of one kind or another—and I use that term broadly, intending to capture everything it is you do for a purpose outside of your primary job—and as already discussed, there is a blending of the personal and the professional in ways previous generations didn't experience.

Many successful people strive to pursue their passions as their careers—or strive to turn their passions into something more than just a hobby—and it misrepresents the way we think about our lives and identities in today's world to draw a crisp line between what we do for work and what we do for leisure. It is not black and white, and the search for a new job is quite often the search for something bigger than that. At the same time, for people who aren't in the traditional workforce—caregivers at home, people who may be retired and still aiming to give back—the way you spend your time is just as valuable and meaningful as for people focused on paid work, full stop.

This chapter is about how to find what to do, whether it's a job or not. To me, it's like solving a math problem. We have a set of dimensions on which we can all make choices, we rank them in order of importance, and then we know what we're aiming for. As the Beatles' George Harrison wrote, in his final single, "Any Road," released after his death, "If you don't know where you're going, any road will take you there." Once we know how we're going to make the decision, we go out and generate options, and then we evaluate those options against our rubric.

HOW TO FIND THE RIGHT OPPORTUNITIES

In a general sense, the right opportunities are found within the intersection of what gives you energy, what you are good at, and what the world needs. In effect, you work through all of the elements and then rank them against each other to figure out what rises to the top. The forced ranking is the first step to creating a pitch: Suppose you have one minute with a potential connector. We never know when we're going to meet the person who will cause an inflection point in our lives. We need to treat everyone like they might be that person—and so we should always be prepared to share what we're looking for.

So many SEALs, for instance, struggle when they transition from the military, because they don't know what they're looking for. They haven't necessarily put in the work to understand what they want out of their next opportunity. The life of a SEAL is so focused on the Short Game of being in the military—*What's your assignment today?*—that there's little room to do the kind of Long Game reflection we've been doing. It's why when SEALs reach out to me asking for guidance on their next steps post-Navy, not knowing where to begin, I'm honest with them that finding the right opportunities is not a five-minute conversation, and that the first step isn't asking for help, it's looking inside yourself to understand what makes you tick.

You're ahead of the game by now, because you've already done that introspection and know your measures of success. You're at a point in the journey where you may know exactly *who* you want to be—but you might still not know how to make it happen.

Knowing who you are is so critical to becoming Mission Driven, but it's not sufficient. Gathering the right next choices—your job, or however else you spend the bulk of your days—is an enormous task, with dozens of variables, and an answer set that isn't always obvious. I've seen too many ex-SEALs start their job search with an open-ended call to their network, hoping an opportunity comes through—but that's a prime example of what I'd call bottom-up thinking. You take the couple of choices you've been given and pick the best of them. Sometimes that's fine, but oftentimes none of what emerges from a haphazard process like that is going to be right. You might end up with a decent job, but is your mission going to emerge from what happens to be top of mind for the people you think to reach out to?

The better way to find what will achieve your mission is far more often top-down: It doesn't matter what opportunities are out there unless they're the right ones. You need to direct the search, know what you're looking for, and take intentional action to generate the very best, most targeted opportunities for you.

I asked the SEAL who emailed me what he was looking for, and he started where so many people do: "I just want to have real impact with an amazing team working on something important." That answer is simultaneously awesome and not helpful. How do you get from there to a useful process? There are six steps to follow:

STEP 1: THINKING ACROSS DIMENSIONS

We start with a set of very concrete dimensions that we all should think about when considering how we put the Long Game into action.

Exercise 7.1

When we look at the person we want to be, what actually matters? There are endless possible answers to that question, but when it comes down to it, I find that most people center on about fifteen concrete decision points, particularly in a job search. This is not an exhaustive list, and other factors may come to mind as you read—and if so, that's great; add them in. The questions after each one aren't exhaustive either, just a starting point to orient your thinking. Some of these may not matter at all to you, and that's a perfect discovery. Some of these may be dispositive and matter more than any others. Terrific, and that's exactly what this exercise is trying to uncover. Answer these questions for yourself—honestly—and then think of any idiosyncratic elements that may be relevant to your own life but missing from this list.

- **Geography:** Where do you want or need to be? If you say you'll go "anywhere," do you mean, in fact, anywhere, or are you envisioning a particular kind of location: big city vs. small town, United States vs. international, Europe vs. Asia, downtown vs. suburban, West Coast vs. East Coast? (I'm not ignoring the potential for remote work, incidentally, but I'll cover that in a different factor below.)
- **Sector:** Is the industry important, building on either past experience or a passion? Is there an industry area where you feel you add outsized value and would like to keep doing so? Are there related industries that build on those skills but offer a closer match for other reasons? Are there sectors you want to avoid because of either past experiences or a lack of interest?

- **Size of firm:** Do you want the camaraderie and all-hands-on-deck nature of a small team, where you could potentially chart your own course, or the opportunity to be part of a large organization that may offer a more predictable role, a clear path upward, and a more established structure within which you would fit? (Alternatively, are you looking to work for yourself—a firm size of one?)

- **Ability to move within the organization:** Do you want to find a place with a hierarchy and a clear career path? Is the expectation that this is a long-term home, or a short-term stop? Do you want to find a place where there are many roles in which you could imagine adding value, or growing into, or are you a solo performer who would be content remaining in the same role for a long time?

- **Quality of life:** How much do you want to be working, and how intense do you want the work to be? Do you want predictable hours? Travel?

- **Quality of people:** Do you care if the people you'll be working with are stars in their own right? Does it matter how much you will be working with them?

- **Compensation:** How much does compensation matter? Are you open to sacrificing present income for future opportunities?

- **Risk:** How important is stability and a guaranteed floor vs. potential upside? This question can be asked on two levels: your own personal risk (bonus vs. salary; stability of your role vs. the possibility of change) and the organization's risk (startup vs. established company; stable industry vs. evolving one).

- **Learning:** Are you looking to gain new knowledge and skills as compared to relying on skills and knowledge you already have?
- **Culture and fun:** What are your expectations as far as fun and enjoyment? Do you want the work, or the workplace, to be enjoyable, and what does that mean to you? What is the right corporate culture for you?
- **Type of role:** There are three types of roles: investors (take someone else's money and make more with it), advisers (help others to be more successful), and operators (lead or run a function to drive a business or a business outcome). Which one do you want to be?
- **Diversity:** Along any axis you choose—gender, religion, age, education, geography, life experience, skill set—what types of diversity are important to you?
- **Meritocracy:** How important is it to you that an organization values the best people the most?
- **Potential for impact:** No matter how you define *impact*, does making an impact matter to you? (No judgment.) And what level of impact will satisfy you? Some people thrive in a setting where they know they're doing work aligned with causes they believe in, and some people are motivated by other factors instead.
- **Connection to the company mission:** There are people who want to be at the center of a firm's core activities, and others whose roles may naturally be more ancillary. How connected to the mission do you need to be?
- **Optics:** How important is it to you that your role and title

"sound cool" (as opposed to how cool they may actually be) when you tell others what you're doing?

- **Engagement with the world:** Are you looking to interact with others, to be a public face, to gain new experiences—or are you okay being more isolated or siloed? I've met wonderfully talented contributors who just want to work at their desks, and others who crave contact, fresh inputs, and a job for an organization regularly making news.

- **Optionality:** Are you concerned about future choices? I had a friend in the SEALs who went to graduate school after his service, and then to a large investment bank to trade precious metals. He was happy, but the job greatly reduced his optionality; the world only needs so many metal traders. It's a fine choice to make, but make it with intention so down the road you don't regret having carved out such a narrow specialty. For the life you want to build in the future, what pieces are you hoping to have in place? What kind of role would make your future goals more difficult to achieve?

- **Freedom and autonomy:** Whether remote or in person, there are vastly different expectations that firms might make on your time. Are you looking for flexibility, and does it matter? Do you want to be judged based on face time or output, and is that important to you?

If there are other dimensions that come to mind for your particular situation—any specific benefits (health care, pension, etc.) that are important, or other factors unique to your life—add them to the list. And please remember there are no right or wrong answers to the questions here. Whenever we get advice from people, almost without exception, they assume that our priorities are the same as theirs. We all imagine ourselves to be the smartest person we know, whose opinions should obviously be listened to and respected—but this presumes that we all derive energy in the same way and have the same wants, needs, and preferences, and that's simply not the case. We are all unique individuals with unique demands and wishes, and this entire exercise is about sorting out what really matters to you, asking yourself questions, and not being biased by other people's answers.

From this exercise, you have the start of a job description—not the kind of job description you would see in an advertisement, but a level up from that, a description of where you want to be with the details yet to be filled in.

STEP 2: FORCE RANKING

This is, as I said, an enormous math problem—and the next step, having done the thinking in Step 1, is to rank the different elements in order of how important they are to you.

Exercise 7.2

Give each individual dimension a score between 0 and 100, with 100 being a dispositive factor that is absolutely going to drive your decision on its own—"I must have a good health care plan"; "the job must be in Cincinnati"; "I don't want to travel"—and 0 for an element that is of no relevance to you. Once you've decided on each of those numbers individually, order your list from 100 down to 0. That is your priority rank list, and the "map" by which you can guide your thinking.

By force ranking, we don't just tell ourselves what's absolutely important, but we see what is relatively important and give ourselves a way to evaluate trade-offs that we will have to make. I went to Bridgewater after the SEALs knowing that I was choosing, just as an example, learning and compensation over quality of life. There were days I wished I hadn't made that choice, for sure—but I could stay even-keeled emotionally because I knew I had made the choice with intention. I don't say that to diminish how hard it was. It was hard, for sure, to be torn apart some days, every decision overanalyzed and questioned. It was terrific training, but if I had gone there thinking that I was going to enjoy every aspect of the role, I would have been crushed to realize it wasn't that kind of place.

I needed to be at peace with the fact I had prioritized growth, even hard growth, over comfort, and trust I could make different choices next time if that's what I decided to do. This, like any opportunity, didn't have to be forever—just like my priorities didn't have to be the same for the rest of my career.

I think about my friend and SEAL teammate Rocky Russell. He works for a small regional insurance company in the state of Florida. My initial instinct when he asked me for advice about taking the job was to say no—it's a bad choice! It's not big enough, it's too risky, and why should he limit his search to Florida, where he was living at the time? But his factors weren't mine, and once we ran through his list—wanting to learn and grow, not move, take asymmetric risk with strong upside (a small bet with the chance of a large reward)—I realized that he was absolutely making the best choice for himself. He was right. The risk paid off. The company is doing quite well, and

Rocky is in a great position—not only to make lots of money in the near term, but to gain solid experience for the longer term.

STEP 3: THE ELEVATOR PITCH

Go all the way back to the first exercise in this book. I asked you to craft your elevator pitch. It was probably not great, at least not yet. But now you finally have all the tools to do much, much better.

Exercise 7.3

Craft your new elevator pitch. But beware—your force ranking isn't enough. This exercise isn't about packing as much information about your rank list into thirty seconds—"I want a job in Cincinnati with great health care and no travel, terrific people I will work closely with, and a flexible schedule that won't require unnecessary face time"—but about telling a specific story about who you want to be, and how you want to get there. You might emerge from the force-ranking exercise with something too detailed, like my example just now. You might also end up with a crisp, clear statement that is impossible to make actionable, such as, "I just want to work with a great team and maximize impact." That's terrific, but no one can help you from that and connect you to a practical conversation. You need to give both of those pitches more life, specificity, and color. Bring the force ranking together with elements of your *who* to result in something like this:

"My number-one priority is to work in financial services—ideally wealth management or the payments space. I'd love a chief of staff role for someone with strong industry experience who would be willing to help me learn, but who could also benefit from and value my strengths in strategy, leadership, and execution. Over time I'd aim toward running a division or line of business, with an eye toward becoming either a chief operating or revenue/growth offi-cer, and eventually running something of my own. I'm completely agnostic when it comes to geography—I'll live anywhere and am ready for the hours and travel that might be necessary."

As soon as I hear something like that, I know where to turn: Who do I know who can help? I'm looking for someone in financial ser-vices who is at the very highest level at a firm that can use someone looking for growth and opportunity. I can almost instantly connect someone who tells me something like that to the next three people they should talk to—which should be the primary aim when you're trying to generate possible opportunities. See, someone like me might have a thousand people in their head to whom they can possibly send you, but the right elevator pitch is what focuses them on the three to five they think are most likely to help you get to your goal.

It's like buying or renting a house. The more descriptive a prop-erty listing is, the more efficient you can be—you quickly know if it's not for you, or whether it's worth a visit. Just like a house listing, your pitch needs to be as crisp as possible. Otherwise you may end up looking at a life with a garden when you really wanted a pool.

Unfortunately, I end up talking to so many people who—even having the opportunity to ask me for help—expect me to be able to guide them in the right direction based on vague parameters. As much as someone wants to help, "I want to do something meaning-ful, and I'll work anywhere" is paralyzing. It provides no real direc-tion. But imagine if you tell me you've made an impact in the SEALs and it helped you understand that for the chance to impact an organization at the highest level, you'll go to any major city on the East Coast, to work with smart people motivated by making a difference either for children or the environment, that you don't care whether it's a for profit or nonprofit, but that it must be in a culture that prioritizes family and flexibility, in a role that lets you interact with lots of interesting individuals around the world. I don't know if I'll know the right person right away, but I might, and I have a lot more to go on than if you just tell me you want to do something meaningful.

The elevator pitch should be designed to allow someone to easily figure out who you should talk to. Where you land is going to be a direct result of what you tell someone you want. Specificity matters. If you tell me that geography is the thing driving you, and that you'll sacrifice what it takes to land in, say, Denver, beyond any other criteria, then I'm going to think of everyone I know who could possibly help you get a job in Denver. But if you just tell me you want to live in a big city, then Denver might never come to mind.

I think about my good friend Tim Boehmer, a talented SEAL and my operations chief when I was an ops officer. He was looking to transition out of the SEALs after a thirty-year career and needed some help. I ran him through this very exercise to give himself clarity on what he wanted. Where it came out: He ended up with a crisp pitch regarding who he was and what he wanted, and realized that his number one priority was to work either in Florida or back in his home state of Iowa. I called a friend, Bruce Rastetter, who has been remarkably successful running Summit Agricultural Group and knows everyone in Iowa. I met Bruce because he was in the audience when I spoke at another friend's annual investor conference.

Bruce asked me to speak at his conference a year later. I described to Bruce what Tim was like and what he was good at, and asked Bruce to help generate some conversations for him. Sure enough, Tim is back home in Iowa and a rock star in his role. I'm sure he could have done something flashier if he'd wanted to live somewhere else, but he landed exactly where he wanted, in a job he wanted—because he had clarity on what he was really looking for.

STEP 4: HAVING THE RIGHT CONVERSATIONS

The preparation you've already done should make the conversations that follow much easier than they would have otherwise been without that early legwork. If you've crafted the right elevator pitch, what comes next should be natural. You want to live in Denver, and I've connected you with someone who knows everyone who's anyone in Denver. So where do you start? You refine that pitch again, because it's going to get you one step closer to the right opportunity.

I categorize conversations about potential opportunities as being on one of three levels:

- Level 1 is general advice.
- Level 2 is with someone who could give you a job.
- Level 3 is a specific conversation about a specific role, in most cases an informal or formal job interview.

People focus on trying to have Level 3 conversations, but the Level 1s are in fact the most crucial. They are the introductions that end up creating the Level 3 conversations that matter. You can think of it like a funnel: The job you end up landing is just a function of everything that goes into that funnel and how you filter along the way. That's why the work really starts with what you're putting into the funnel in the first place, enabled by your own pitch and the Level 1 conversations you create.

We also never know when what we think is a Level 1 conversation will immediately turn into a Level 2 or Level 3. The words you say might happen to click, and suddenly someone knows not only the right person you should talk to but also the perfect job—and, it turns out, they're the one hiring for it, or they happen to know who's hiring and are moved to help you land the role.

The way we change our lives is to *motivate others to extend themselves on our behalf.* Too often, we are reactive rather than proactive: We look at the options presented to us instead of asking whether those are, in fact, the options we ought to be choosing from. But there are no limits in this world, except those we place upon ourselves. You are one conversation away from fixing pretty much any mistake you might have ever made. Maybe you made the wrong choice years ago and pursued the wrong degree, or your first job was, in retrospect, not the optimal one. Are you stuck? Perhaps in the short term—you have bills to pay—but no one is stuck forever. You can go back to school, start a side hustle, or embark on something entirely different. And when you can effectively articulate your goal, others can help you unlock it. The most successful people know that life is a team sport.

The way I approach any conversation is with an open mind. If someone has agreed to meet with you, there's a reason. And you do want to very directly ask what those reasons are. When someone offers to connect you to someone they know, it is not at all inappropriate to ask what made them think of that person. "I thought of Janet because she used to be in the same industry and might know someone" may mean a different conversation than "Janet's hiring for a role in her group," or "Janet's looking for the same kinds of opportunities you are, and I thought you might hit it off," or "Janet has no experience that I know of in your industry, but she's the best connector I know, bar none, and I'm sure there's someone in her network who can point you in the right direction."

You may worry about the position someone has in a particular organization—should you, perhaps as someone very junior, be talking to a CEO, or conversely, should you, as someone quite senior in your career, bother talking to a mid-level manager? I tell people not to worry about any of it—you never know who will have great advice, or who can lead you in the right direction. At the same time, very few people, from a practical perspective, would ever say, "Yes, I think you'd be perfect for that role...as my boss." So as you get closer to Level 2 and Level 3 conversations, it does often make sense to talk to the highest-level individuals you can, and not expect that opportunities will emerge from people at more junior levels. That doesn't mean the connections and conversations can't be useful, though.

Incidentally, sometimes the connector you're looking for is... you. You may have met someone in the past and had what you didn't realize at the time was a Level 1 conversation. Perhaps you didn't need anything back then, but could use some help now. It is never too late to reach back out and reconnect with someone. I remember back when I was a White House Fellow and met Jamie Dimon, chairman and CEO of JPMorganChase. He told me that he'd be

happy to help whenever I decided to leave the SEALs and was looking for a new opportunity. I was struck by his sincerity. Three years
had elapsed, and I hadn't kept in contact with him—I was overseas
in Afghanistan and why in the world would Jamie Dimon want to
hear from me? But the right email can reactivate someone. You need
to remind someone who you are and where they met you—reanchor
them in the good feelings they had when they offered to help in the
first place—and then, you might find yourself in a useful conversation right away:

In my note to him, I reminded him very specifically who I was
and where we'd met:

> *Mr. Dimon,*
> *You gave a tremendous talk to my White House Fellows class in*
> *2008. After our follow-up conversation, you asked me to reach*
> *out when I was ready to transition out of the SEAL Teams. I am*
> *currently the Commanding Officer of SEAL Team TWO and*
> *recently returned from nine months in Afghanistan in charge*
> *of a 2000-person Special Operations Task Force. I will soon*
> *complete 20 years of service in the SEALs and plan to transition*
> *to the private sector in the late spring/early summer....*

But when I look back on that email from more than a decade
ago, I cringe a little, because I didn't do what I preach in this book,
and what I would do if I were writing it again today. I should have
been far clearer.

"I'm now looking for an opportunity in the private sector,"
I might have said, "preferably on the East Coast, where I could

use my experience as a White House Fellow combined with my military leadership experience to help drive outcomes within a financial services company that's looking for someone who can motivate internal leaders and clients alike, ideally within asset management, consumer and community banking, or corporate and investment banking."

A note like that would have helped him more easily help me and hopefully think about opportunities—whether at JPMorganChase or elsewhere—that might be a fit.

Sometimes you get lucky. He wrote back to me an hour later and said, "I'd be happy to get together on one of your upcoming trips to New York. Call my office directly to set it up." I set up a meeting for as soon as I could, and got myself to New York—but I look back at his response now and so greatly appreciate what it really says: *I know you're getting out of the SEALs and you don't totally know what you want. We're always hiring general athlete-type top talent. I'll meet you and then ask my team to help figure out if something might make sense within JPMorganChase.*

I capitalized on the opening—and we'll get to meeting preparation in a moment—but I know now that I could have done so much more to help myself in that initial message, not just by being clearer about what I was looking for, but also by approaching it from the mindset I've been preaching throughout these pages and trying to help *him* before I asked for help for me. What could I have offered Jamie Dimon as a SEAL about to transition out? I wasn't sure at the time, but that's the kind of thinking I should have been more focused on, not just asking him for a favor. But we're all always learning, and all we can do is our best at the time. And another, perhaps larger, point—not lost on me in the business world: There's no one busier than Jamie Dimon, but somehow he found and made time to help me. Jamie set the example we should all follow.

On to preparation: The kind of preparation to do for any meeting depends a bit on what the expectations are. If you think there's a chance the person may have a job to offer, then it will never hurt to read up on their company and learn everything you can. If the person is being pitched to you as a great connector, it's not a bad idea to look at their LinkedIn page and see who they know, just in case you see someone you specifically would love to speak with. I should add, though, that no matter how much research you do, your most important task in a meeting is to find the line between moving a conversation in a particular direction and letting it feel as organic as possible. If you discover the person you're about to talk to knows the head of a particular division at, say, Google, where you'd love to work, I would suggest that you not lead with that information and force the conversation to go there. If it comes up, that's great. But forcing things never really works. You never know the thoughts in someone else's head, how they feel about their connection at Google, or about you, or about their ability or interest in making or not making that match. Let things unfold the way they unfold. Just keep what you know in the back of your mind.

What you're really looking for in these conversations is what's called product-market fit in business—except here, you're the product. And if everyone you talk to is steering you toward a great opportunity in the education sector—even if you've never thought about being a teacher—then either your elevator pitch is pushing you to the wrong place, or maybe that's in fact something you should consider.

It turns out that when you have great product-market fit, the market often finds you without much effort—but if the fit is not quite there, it can be really hard to push a rock up a hill. You may want to work at Google, but if no one you talk to thinks that makes sense, you are probably not going to end up at Google!

Mechanically, in every conversation, you should save your ask until the end. Exhaust the advice of the person you're with before you make any asks at all. Get everything from them, because much of it may be quite useful, and then, when the conversation is wrapping up, ask two things:

- First, how's my pitch? Get their feedback. If they tear it apart, ask if you can try again in forty-eight hours, and run a new version by them. More likely, they'll say it's great, and then you can still ask them one thing you can do to improve it.
- Second, who are two to three people you think I should talk to? Ask why those people, so you know what to expect from the meetings, and then you're off to have some more conversations.

Eventually, you will land on the person with the opportunity for you—it's inevitable if you do this right, and talk to enough people—but you do need patience, because it almost never happens right away.

Finally, it can't hurt as you prepare for any of these conversations to think, again, not just about how someone might be able to help you, but about how you might be able to help them—think back to the lesson in chapter 4: Helping others helps us more. In fact, you should ask outright. End each conversation by expressing how much you appreciate the help, and then make a genuine offer, asking what you can do for the person who has just given you their time and energy.

I find that junior people often think there's nothing they can do for a senior person, but that's just not true (or if the senior person thinks that's true, then the problem is him/her!). Everyone who is more senior should always work to stay connected to the younger/more junior perspectives of the workplace. For example, my generation (Gen X) was not born digital. My daughter's generation (Gen Z) are digital natives. I can't tell you how many times I've learned fascinating insights from Gen Z that make me a better Gen X business leader. I was at a conference recently where the speaker pointed out that there are now more Gen Zers in the workplace than Boomers. The speaker showed how different the generations are when it comes to using the phone: For Gen Zers, phones aren't for speaking. They're for DMing, texting, and, when they're thinking about buying something, getting opinions based on six-second TikToks and the company's Instagram page. Of course, by the time you read this, all of this may have already changed!

Even if the senior person doesn't have an ask now, knowing you have one more person in the world who will help you is always awesome, irrespective of age or seniority. When you consistently aspire to give more than you get, the world will eventually come your way.

STEP 5: THE FOLLOW-UP

I'm going to be blunt here: I can judge who will be successful by whether they ghost me after I send them networking leads, or if they come back and say thank you. It's a real proxy for the kind of performer someone is in the world. Think about it: Do you want to help people who don't say thank you, or who let you know if and how your help paid off? Someone who doesn't circle back might win anyway, and get what they want in the short term, but it's the Long Game that really matters—and even if they seem successful from the outside, you never know how much more someone could have accomplished if only they were more aware and explicitly thankful.

Teachers live for the positive notes they get from past students. (And how hard is it to write one nice note every month or year to say thank you?) These kinds of notes don't have to be long:

Hey, Mrs. Wardenburg—It's been years since I was in your class, but I just wanted to let you know that you were a tremendously meaningful influence on me as I was growing up. I honestly can't remember a thing you taught in the class. What I remember is that I was always challenged, learned a lot, and loved being around you. What you did for me, which I never recognized at the time, was serve as an example of how I want to be as an adult. If I can give back even a portion to the world that you've given, I'll consider myself successful. Thank you for being such a great positive influence on me! Sincerely, Mike

Imagine how much better the world would be if we could all slow down for sixty seconds now and then to say thank you. We all want to know what we've done has made a difference. And if we want people to continue to keep us in mind, it's critical to focus on nurturing those relationships, keeping people in your circles, updating them on where you are and how you're doing, and at the same time, asking how you can be of service to them.

As you trace your way through the conversations you have with people, you should always circle back and tell the person who made the introduction what happened. Part of that is for the humanity of it, so that it didn't feel like a useless effort from the person who took the time to help, and so they stay invested and know that their help was appreciated and used. But part of it is also to guide further help. If someone comes back to me and not only thanks me for an intro, but tells me that the conversation sparked some more specific thinking—"Now I know I want to work in financial services for sure, and would expand my geographic parameters to do so"—then I might be able to give them some new, more targeted leads, or connect them to other people who may not have originally come to mind.

At the same time, they might tell me the conversation didn't produce much in the way of progress, because they realized they're looking for something more creative, or with more learning, and exploring one particular direction made them change their force rank. That's helpful, too, and I can think of a few additional people for them to talk to instead:

Hey, just a quick note to say thank you so much for the intro to XYZ. We had a great conversation and it's super easy to see why you think so highly of her. She is going to keep me in mind, but we didn't have any concrete next steps. If you're inclined to think of anyone else and it isn't too hard for you, I have capacity for a few more conversations.

The best way to do this is with a handwritten note—perhaps especially in this digital age. It stands out, and it makes a difference.

If you look at conversations as being the start of a dialogue and not just a one-and-done point in time, then you create a funnel that keeps growing and expanding. Fill it with positive energy and goodwill, not just to keep it from feeling too transactional, but because it can help you. And even if it doesn't help you now, it might in the future.

I helped Frank D'Souza by speaking to his leadership team from my role in the White House in 2009. Eight years later, I joined the fourteen-person leadership team of his 350,000-person Fortune 200 firm. Things can take time to develop. I didn't help Frank because I was hoping to one day get something from him—that was the last thing on my mind when I said "yes"—but if you are long on meaning and impact, things have a way of working out well in the end.

STEP 6: MAKING THE CHOICE

This entire process is hopefully getting you to a point where you have choices. You can't make a decision until you have options, and more and more targeted conversations should eventually lead to those options. It is absolutely the case that you can't and shouldn't search forever. No one can possibly optimize the equation and get to the perfect answer. Again, it's like buying a house. No house is perfect, and you could look at houses forever if you wanted to. There will always be a desire for one more bedroom or the better school district. But you can keep going back to your map and decide if you've found something that is right in enough ways that it is good for now.

As a SEAL Teammate and close friend named Dave described what he was looking for, it took me zero point six seconds to know exactly what he should do. I made introductions and moved out of the way. The hard question for Dave, after he met the team, was whether he should jump at the first opportunity in front of him. My advice 99% of the time is no—of course not! Go look at more things! But in this case, it was an obvious fit, and sometimes you just have to follow your gut. Why spend time looking for more when the thing in front of you ticks almost all of your boxes?

Your force ranking should make it easy. And to some degree it also helps you in the future because it's harder to harbor resentment when you can look back and know you made an active choice. "I didn't prioritize culture," you might realize, "and I'm disappointed by the way people here work together—but I decided compensation was more important." When things unfold as predicted, it's not a surprise. So much of the stress and grind of a bad job is about the difference between what you expected and what you get. But if you knew what you were choosing, there's less room for dissatisfaction.

It is hard not to second-guess yourself. I think about a colleague who was recently faced with two options for his next move, one job that would pay a significant salary and still allow him the flexibility to spend time with his family, and another job that was even more lucrative, with more responsibility and more growth potential, but that would likely keep him away from home most of the time. His priorities were clear: He wanted a life where his kids would know him, and where he could be a constant presence at home. So the choice was clear—but that still didn't make it easy. Deciding to pass up what many might think of as the "bigger" job was hard, and he hemmed and hawed until he had to pull the trigger.

I can go back again to my decision to work at Bridgewater. The honest truth of it is that very quickly after starting, I realized it wasn't a place where I was going to want to stay long term. There was a lot I knew I could get out of the experience, but I also knew I didn't want to do it for the rest of my life. I committed to myself that I would stay for at least two years, because I knew anything less than two years wouldn't give me a real experience from which to extract enough learning and make career judgments that would set me up for future success. Putting that on the calendar—telling myself I would move on after two years—gave me the freedom to fully invest myself in what I was doing, knowing it was temporary. (Remember, nothing is permanent.) It helped me be happier in trying moments. It also freed me to look for what was next without feeling pressure to leave immediately and say "yes" to the very first opportunity that presented itself.

As I said earlier, you never want to merely run away from something—you want to run *to* something else, with clear reasons why it's your next stop and not just an excuse to move past something that isn't necessarily working. I ended up at Bridgewater for three and a half years. It took a full eighteen months after the two-year point for me to find the perfect next step—and I was impatient, for sure (once again, I'm terrible at patience)—but it was time that was worth spending in order to make the next move the right one, and when I look back on my time at Bridgewater, I'm filled with extreme gratitude for so much learning from top-notch colleagues and many lifelong friends.

You have to live in two worlds at once: While you're trying to find your next thing, you also have to be a professional and perform where you are. In fact, I probably learned more in my last eighteen months at Bridgewater than I did in my first two years. There was no better place to grow my skills as a leader, even if it was intense in the wrong ways or just plain not fun.

And I should say—I may make transitions sound easy, but I know they're super hard. I want to be in control and fix everything—now. But you need the self-control to understand that not everything is instant, and the best option may involve a bit of waiting.

In the end, having a framework helps you make the best choice at the time—and then you move on when you need to, knowing that you did everything you could to make the decision process the best it could be.

NOT JUST ABOUT JOBS

This chapter is about time, and your time concerns more than just your job. People sometimes look at my life and think it seems far too crowded. I have a full-time job, I'm on the boards of private companies and nonprofits, I've written books, I give talks, and I make a point to carve out dedicated time with my wife and daughter. People get scared of adding things to their life beyond their "traditional" job, but adding a second thing—a nonprofit, a hobby, a side hustle—isn't like going from a 1x amount of work to 2x. If you add the right thing, it's accretive to your primary role, not entirely separate.

What do I mean by that? It's not just the point I made in chapter 4, about service still counting as service even when it helps you, too. It's bigger than that. When I give talks, they benefit the primary work I do, they benefit the book writing, they benefit the nonprofit work, and they sometimes even provide an excuse for a few vacation days with my family. Even the thinking I do to prepare for a talk is thinking that benefits me elsewhere, and the conversations the talk may spark often fold back into my job by generating a new customer or investor or someone who will provide an internship to my teammate's son. If you pick the right additional things to do in life, the work goes from $1x$ to $1.1x$ while the value jumps from $1x$ to $3x$.

I don't mean to scare anyone off with the math. Let me say it a different way: The amount of work we have to do will fill the space we provide it. If you need more mission in your life—if you haven't found enough—it may just be that you're spending all of your energy on something that doesn't quite need it. You shouldn't be afraid to bring more activities and opportunities into your life, inside or outside your primary job, because benefits will emerge and things will rarely take as much extra energy and time as you fear.

If you know what motivates you—and after reading this chapter, I hope you do—then you can pick things that give you energy and fuel your fire. Things, in other words, that help move you closer to living a Mission Driven life.

In the next chapter, we'll move from work to relationships, and talk about how the same principles that enable you to find the best next opportunity can also help you identify the people with which to fill your life and carry you along on the journey toward your mission.

CHAPTER EIGHT

Mission Driven in Our Relationships

My friend Job Price and I used to joke that together we made one heck of a good SEAL. Between the two of us, he had the on-the-fly creativity, humor, and flexibility to counter the sometimes-too-intense focus and preparation I would default to. It wasn't exactly that we were opposites, but we brought out the best elements of each other, which is why we weren't just good teammates, but people who genuinely enjoyed each other's company.

Job sadly died by suicide on his last deployment, a story that was covered by the *New York Times* and that I shared in *Never Enough*. The short version is that our families were intertwined; the lines between our work and our lives blurred; my daughter tried to help his daughter make it through the difficult period after the unthinkable occurred; and I made it my mission to support his family however I could.

Our mission does not end when we clock out for the day, if we even clock out at all. A Mission Driven life is a life where you're all in, where what you do at any given point in the day matters, where your work is something you love, and so the people you do it with become the people you love, too. For many of us, living in siloed lives, our friends busy and sometimes drifting away, time for social connections hard to find, forming and holding on to tight bonds can seem unattainable. But your *who* almost certainly doesn't push you to be someone alone in the world; rather, you almost certainly want to be someone who is part of a community, a family, and a society.

It doesn't just happen. Finding the people to be in the foxhole with you takes no less effort or intention than finding the right ways to spend your time. Which is why the title of this chapter parallels the previous one. It is not enough to be Mission Driven in what you do; we must be Mission Driven in who we do it with, in who we partner with throughout the day, from colleagues to friends to the closest people in our lives. This should not be taken to mean that the people we spend time with need to be on the same professional mission as we are—my wife and most of my closest friends are not—but they should be additive to that mission rather than pulling us away from it; they should support and amplify our efforts rather than detract from them; they should give us strength to push even harder rather than divert our energy and drive us away. They should invest in us as we invest in them, and together we can make all of our collective missions greater and more meaningful.

You may be nodding your head, but when I say that this means we need to force-rank different attributes to make the right choices about who we spend time with, just as we did to figure out the right opportunities to pursue, some of you may pause. It is perhaps unsurprising that we are able to turn the search for jobs or other opportunities into a checklist of sorts. But this is not how we tend to approach our relationships—whether romantic partners or friends. There's something off-putting—perhaps for good reason—about imagining someone grading you against a checklist when deciding whether, say, to date you. We are all three-dimensional individuals, after all, irreducible to a set of mere characteristics. If I introduced you to someone who met every requirement on any checklist you wanted to create, there is, of course, no guarantee that you would "click" with that person, that you'd feel any kind of spark or connection. Relationships simply don't work that way. People connect sometimes in the most unexpected pairings.

And yet I would argue that conceptually the decision process for finding a friend, a business partner, or a spouse shouldn't be all that different. We need to know what we're looking for in order to effectively find it. There are those of us who gain energy from spending time with people who agree with us and support us in whatever ways they can; there are others who gain energy from debate and disagreement, from having a sparring partner. There's no right or wrong, but if you don't know which category you fall into, you run the risk of surrounding yourself with people who won't ultimately give you the energy you need. It is critical to understand what you want from people—and if you're not getting what you need, it's really hard to give it to others. Think about the familiar advice from flight attendants: Put your own oxygen mask on first. (Just like the oxygen toxicity issue mentioned earlier, the first symptom of a lack of oxygen can be unconsciousness—so you really do have to take care of yourself to make sure you can take care of the people around you.)

If, for instance, you are free-spirited, you might find that you thrive around other free spirits and are held back by people who want to plan and decide things well in advance. Or you might need exactly that kind of organized, rigid person to balance you out. Or imagine one partner holding extreme partisan views. Some people like that could never spend their life with someone from the opposite party, but others crave being around someone who holds different opinions and is up for a life of sharp, impassioned debate.

We are all different. And yet whether we're talking about a partner, a friend, or a colleague, the questions are much the same. This book is about being proactive in every aspect of our lives, at least where we can. And, I should add, we can't always choose our professional colleagues—though evaluating who they are and how we fit with them should be part of the process of figuring out if any particular opportunity is right for us. But we can, to some extent (excluding the family we were born into, of course), choose the people with whom we want to spend time in many other aspects of our life. The people around us make or break us. Unlike when it comes to a job or a volunteer opportunity, the commitments are sometimes harder to disentangle, making it that much more critical to choose wisely from the start.

PEOPLE WHO ARE THE SAME/PEOPLE WHO ARE DIFFERENT

Greg Jensen and I worked closely with each other at Bridgewater and became great friends. He was the brains there, the "thinking" side of the spectrum, as opposed to the "feeling" side, and what made it work is he knew that and embraced it. He had a thorough understanding of himself. And that's important. You need to understand who you are—do you make decisions based on your gut or on data, on relationships or on facts? I used to tell Ray Dalio, Bridgewater's founder, that he has an IQ of a million and an EQ of zero…but not to worry because I have an IQ of zero and an EQ of a million, so together we make one great professional!

I could have said that just as easily to Greg. His raw intellectual horsepower and analytical skills were unmatched, but it made him better to surround himself with people like me, who came at things from a different perspective. And being around him made me so much better, too. In any endeavor—in any life—you need some of each, for sure, the thinking and the feeling. Really, you need some of everything. To get there, you have to surround yourself with people who aren't the same as you on all kinds of continuums, because that's how you grow and learn and experience more than you would on your own—and generate the widest range of ideas and inputs.

Think about the mix of people you enjoy being around. It is likely exactly that: a mix. And it should be a mix that tilts in the direction of what you wish you were more like. In many ways, we're the average of the people we hang around with. Which means it's not enough to surround yourself with people who are different. They have to be different from you in ways that excite you, and different in ways that make you better. Job and I collectively made a good SEAL. Greg and I made a good Bridgewater leader. Who do you match with? What kind of person do you need in order to effectively identify and brainstorm problems—and together solve them? I don't mean you need to necessarily find people who are each entirely different from you in all respects—you need common ground and ways to build connection—but you should try to find the sweet spot where there are ways you are the same along with enough different elements to make you a complementary pair. (And we'll get to an exercise around this topic later in this chapter.)

Differences challenge us and help us learn new things. I'm more curious when I'm around people who are speaking a language I don't speak, literally or figuratively. I'm talking about artists, scientists, historians, lawyers, people who play in different worlds than I do and can bring their knowledge, experience, and way of thinking to bear in all of their interactions.

This is one of the reasons I thoroughly enjoy a dinner group I started. I modeled it after John Whitehead's breakfast group that I mentioned earlier. I was in my early forties when I left the SEALs and moved to Westport, Connecticut, to start working at Bridgewater. I knew all of these standout people in New York City, but rarely had an excuse to see them. I thought about the eight, ten, twelve people I knew who were all individually remarkably accomplished but, more importantly, human beings of great character, who embodied the giving attitude I explained in chapter 4. From different industries, different backgrounds, different ages, different religions, different political ideologies, different roles, there would be great benefit to them all knowing each other—and I wanted to see much more of them. I reached out to each of them and told them to commit to the first Tuesday of the month—to put it on their calendar, don't travel, don't make other plans, just trust me. They did. And for almost a decade, we've met up once a month, as many of us who can make it. The group has changed my life and I'm confident saying that everyone else in it would all assert the same thing. I started it at a point in my life when I was craving deeper friendships, and I'm so glad I did.

We used to take turns assigning a reading—an article about the difference between meaning and happiness, say, or what happens if leaders don't carve out time for themselves, or a new angle on servant leadership—just to shape the conversation, but lately we don't even need it. We go around the table giving three-to-five-minute updates on our lives, and then find ourselves talking and sharing and relating. Frank D'Souza reminds us that what we have can't be replicated: "You can't make new old friends." We are all so close. It's really hard to prioritize a monthly dinner, especially for busy people who are often traveling for work, but we have one rule: If you're not traveling, you come. And we do, because it is important. Or more than important—it's vital to each of our lives.

We love coming together and channeling our collective wisdom (or lack thereof!) to talk through each other's monthly updates and help each other with no expectation of receiving anything in return. Or maybe more accurately, to try to help each other to best help others. Wisdom, just like the kinds of meta-skills we talked about earlier, is transferable across different spaces. You don't have to be an expert in someone else's industry to help with 99% of the things they're dealing with. Problems and opportunities tend to be industry agnostic—the field doesn't matter. Helping others translates everywhere. The details may be different, but the problems themselves are almost always the same as we've all faced: Problems only come in so many varieties.

At our dinners, we talk about the challenges or the opportunities we see in the world and get the perspective of smart outsiders who bring their own experiences, ideas, and resources to the table. These conversations have helped each of us over the years, sometimes just by listening and hearing how others are thinking, and other times more tangibly. It's hard to predict, as one of us starts talking, who is going to have the most useful thing to say in response. And my most important observation is that no one has ever come to the group and asked for anything for themselves. We do not even let each other ask for the help they know—or don't know—they need. We say yes before the question arises, or sometimes we even tell each other what is needed when they don't yet realize it. Anytime any of us does ask for anything, it is always in service of someone else.

We should all have groups like this in our lives. Here, in fact, is how to create one.

Exercise 8.1

Pick out the person in your life you most admire—the first one who pops in your head as you've been reading this section is probably perfect, someone local to you but not someone you live with or see all the time; the reason you admire them isn't important. Call them up or drop them a note, or perhaps just send them a picture of this page of the book. Say: Let's start something together, which can lift us both up.

Once a month, let's meet for dinner.

Tell them to pick the person they admire most, and invite them, too. If it's you (and of course it's you!), have them pick the runner-up. Have that person add a person. And have that person add a person, until there are six to ten of you—no more than that, since you want it to be a one-conversation table. Find a day that works for most if not all of you, and schedule your very first dinner.

It may take a few tries to get a group that's the right mix—people will drop off naturally, no need to force it—but soon enough, you'll have your very own team of allies and thought partners to help you tackle the toughest problems you face. And yes, do this—today. It will change your life, and theirs.

FRIENDS AND PROFESSIONAL FRIENDS: ALL THE SAME

Are my monthly dinners networking events or friendship opportunities? They are both, and there's nothing wrong with that. Of course, when I say that, I feel the need to run from the traditional idea of networking, where you're trying to make connections from a self-interested point of view. Back again to the orientation explained in chapter 4, these aren't events to get something from—they're opportunities for you to give. The giving may pay off someday in tangible ways, or it may not, but that's not the point. None of us who are at these dinners would say they're networking events. We're friends, and we're helping each other. And most importantly, we're helping each other to help others.

There are people who may be uncomfortable with the idea that the problems we talk about are often—not always—professional ones, and we sometimes—not often—do intersect in our professional lives. Some people say they want to leave work at work and escape from it when they're not in the office. To me, this is more of an indictment of the culture of their workplace and the people they work with than anything else. It's okay when work friends become real friends, and I love when that happens. Maybe it's because any boundaries at all get erased when you're a SEAL or anything analogous. We are literally among our colleagues exclusively for months: They see us first thing in the morning, last thing at night, at our best, at our worst, and there are no boundaries. To me that's not a bad thing. The blurring of lines between friends and colleagues makes life richer to me. Everywhere I've worked, I've made friends—sometimes they're people I know I'll stay in touch with forever, and sometimes they're not, and either way, it's okay—we all have different needs at different times, and want to be able to call on a range of people. We can cultivate relationships so that those people are there if we need them, and some of them will go beyond "professional friends" to become actual friends. So much of relationship development is simply spending time around a person. It's natural some of those will emerge from work, because we spend a lot of time working.

Regardless of whether someone is our friend because we grew up down the street from them or because they were our boss, we all need to invest in those relationships so we don't get to a point where we haven't talked to someone in "forever" and it would now be awkward to drop them a text out of the blue.

If you are at that point, by the way—don't let "awkward" get in the way! Think about how you would feel hearing from the person you remember passing notes to in your eleventh grade math class. (Speaking of—I haven't spoken to Tim Galvin since maybe high school—Tim, if you're reading, I owe you a call!)

Exercise 8.2

Just do it. Think of five people you wish you hadn't lost touch with. Drop them a text, an email, a letter in the mail—anything. Reach out. Tell them you were thinking of them. There is literally no downside. This book will still be here when you get back.

Relationships will fill your cup and pay dividends professionally but also give you energy and joy in a way that only human connections can. Sometimes a great coffee with a friend is the only thing that can give you that kind of energy. There is a level of time investment involved in building and maintaining relationships, but the payback is so much greater. People undervalue what it means to have people in your life who push and inspire you. Be open to those people—and be that person for others. Reach out in big moments, but reach out in little ones, too.

In fact, a few years ago, I envisioned something along these lines that the world needed but that didn't exist. I was involved in launching Ren, an app that pulls one clean set of your contacts from all your platforms and reads the entire internet all the time to surface what is happening in the lives of the people in your network. It then makes it super easy to "reach out in the moments that matter." In short, it surfaces news about friends or professional colleagues that you wouldn't have otherwise seen, and helps you take action because of it. Ren is named after the Confucian value of altruism. For many of us, it's really hard to stay connected to our network and even just to know what people are doing. Ren is like Google Alerts on fire, pulling relevant news and stories that appear in legitimate sources online about friends and businesses you already know. By surfacing these stories, the app makes it easy to congratulate people in your network or check in on a bad day.

I think about my friend Jimmy Graham, who was named Citizen of the Month in his hometown of Nowheresville, Colorado, an honor announced in a tiny local newspaper. Jimmy was a combat hero for me in the SEALs. Amid our enemy firing at us, he rigged a radio antenna that helped us contact helicopters that saved our entire team in Kosovo. I saw the Ren alert and picked up the phone and called him. I left Jimmy a voicemail saying, "Jim—you might be the hero of the month in your one-horse town, but you're also my hero for life." He had no idea how I saw that article, and it didn't matter. It was an excuse to reach out, and his reaction when he called me back reminded me: Little things have impact.

The digital world has made things both easier and harder. We can be connected to so many people—but are we really connected to them? Not unless we make sure we are and focus on maintaining those ties.

Especially in a mentoring position where you are some number of levels "above" someone in a hierarchy (though, again, in reality no one is ever above or below anyone else), people look up to you. We naturally look up to the people more senior than we are, and we think they have some special wisdom—but being on the other end now, I have to tell you that we don't. In our minds, we are still the same people we always were.

In my roles now, I constantly have to remind myself that little things matter and people appreciate being noticed by me even if I don't really understand why. There is power to being senior in an organization. I can make someone's day with a word of praise. It takes two seconds for me, but it matters. I still remember how much I looked up to my commanding officers as a SEAL. I was twenty-two years old and trying my best to be elite, to hide my imperfections (I could not for the life of me master the pull-up bar). Almost two decades later, I was the same guy (I still cheat on my pull-ups and in my own mind tell myself I can do more than I really can), but now instead of looking up to someone else, people were looking up to me.

And I kept having to remind myself that I was no different. It was just my situation that was different. The new guys looked up to us in the way we used to look up to others.

This relates to another point—there is a transition in life, and maybe some readers are there and some aren't quite yet—when you become someone too senior to get compliments. No one wants to seem like they're brown-nosing their boss and telling them what a great job they're doing. But even the bosses need that, I promise. It's nice to feel like people like you, no matter how senior you are. We assume the people in charge know their value, but they may not, and we all sometimes need to be reminded. Reaching down, reaching up, reaching across—these are all ways to build stronger relationships. Maybe it starts out as transactional, but you never know where it will end up. Not to mention, if you establish a relationship now, with positive affirmations, it gives you an opening to perhaps one day share critical feedback if you need to. Give the right feedback in the right moment. Criticism is much better to take when it comes from someone you already know, like, and trust.

And a secret from a senior leader: When you get into conversations with more junior employees, talk about your vacations, because it's a signal to your team that you give them permission to take breaks, too. And ask about their breaks. People who don't take sufficient breaks aren't as productive, and when people can't tell you what they're doing or where they're going on their next break, it means they haven't really planned a break. The best thing I can do as a leader is make someone describe their vacation plans. If they have nothing to say, I call them out—to help them. Honestly, I'm not always great at vacation planning myself, and when someone does this to me, it's an awesomely helpful reminder.

In chapter 7, I wrote about the specific power of handwritten notes after an interview. But notes aren't just for work. On a personal level, a note is a thrilling thing to receive. We should all write more notes to people. Taking the time to do that can really have an impact. A note is such a nice thing to get. In the White House Fellows, we had to send a handwritten note to every speaker who came to share their story with us. This time-honored tradition built great habits, and it built relationships. Once you get in the habit, it's not hard to do. We had 200 speakers and I wrote 200 notes. It was useful practice for the rest of my life.

Exercise 8.3

Who has made an impact on you today? Who can you send a note to—and make their day? Reach out to the author of the article you just read, the one that moved you—and make a connection. There's no better time to start than right now.

PERSONAL RELATIONSHIP FORCE RANKING

Just as we did for opportunities and jobs in chapter 7, we can go through a list of questions when it comes to relationships, force-rank those elements, and then evaluate the people in our lives against them. Again, this may not be an exhaustive list. You may feel drawn to, say, fellow bird-watchers, and want to spend time with them—so that may be an element you add in. But take some time to reflect upon the people you have gotten the most from. Think about the qualities they have in common, the ways they are different, and the roles they have filled for you. Of course, unlike with a job, there's not the same kind of pressure to have one person fill all the buckets for you. You can't really have two full-time jobs—you can combine different roles and opportunities, for sure, but time, energy, and flexibility become limiting factors. On the other hand, you can certainly have a dozen friends who each give you something different.

Even your spouse or partner doesn't have to check all the boxes. Relationships are so different from each other: There are spouses who are joined at the hip, aligned in business and in life, and there are other pairs who live very separate lives during the day and then come together and use each other for rest and recharge. There is no right or wrong, certainly. So use this less as a rubric for finding your one true friend and more as a set of qualities you want to better understand in yourself so you know what roles the people in your life might be able to fill, where you might derive energy from them, and where you might struggle.

- **Extroversion/introversion:** Would you rather go to a party with a bunch of people you don't know, or order takeout with one person you already do? And do you gravitate toward people who are inclined similarly or differently? If you're an introvert, do you need people in your life to pull you out of your shell and force you into lively situations, or would you rather spend time with people who don't mind a lazy afternoon on the couch? If you're an extrovert, do you crave people who match your social energy, or do you prefer people who insist on one-on-one time and try to push deeper in your relationship?

- **Comfort doing new things:** Would you rather repeatedly do the things you love (i.e., keep getting better at wakesurfing), or be pushed to do things out of your comfort zone (i.e., learn a new language; join a friend on an around-the-world cruise)? This is different from extroversion/introversion because it's about the activities and not the social piece. You can be an introvert who loves to surf, an extrovert who loves your book club, and everything in between. The question here is whether you are drawn to people who push for novelty and adventure, bringing you into their passions, or want to join you in yours.

- **Drive for impact:** Suppose you won the lottery. Would you still work? Would you withdraw from society and buy a beach house on an island somewhere? Would you dive deeper into volunteer efforts? Would you keep driving toward your business goals? Do you find reward in being around hard-drivers executing their own missions, or people who are more laid-back and don't feel that same pressure in their downtime? Do you like talking about work—yours or someone else's—and helping to brainstorm solutions? Or do you prefer to keep your worlds separate and have people you can just bond with over sports or reality television?

- **Health:** Is your health, however you define it, physical or mental, an area that you want to deal with on your own, or a place where you want company and support? Do you like to find people who share your fitness goals and activities, or is this not something important to you?

- **Intellectual fulfillment:** How vital is being able to discuss and/or debate the headline-making topics in the news, or being with people who have a deep understanding of particular issues in the world or in society? Does it matter to you if they agree or disagree with you on these issues? There are those of us who don't want to be in a constant political debate, others who thrive on that energy, and some who would rather ignore the topic entirely.

- **Humor:** Everyone needs to laugh, but how much do you seek out people who laugh at the same things as you do? Are you sometimes bothered or offended by the jokes of others, and if so, is it important to you to find people who won't push those buttons?

- **Service:** What is your orientation toward giving and service? Do you take on projects alone, or look for others to join you in those efforts?

These are some of the areas I think about in my own life—and why my dinner group is so important to me. I thrive on substantive discussions about work issues, and always want to find ways to help. I thrive being with other connectors who are inclined to bring me along—to meet new people, to have new experiences. And yet, at the same time, I love having a partner who grounds me and doesn't let me constantly perseverate about work and the state of the world, but sometimes just wants to laugh at a movie with me. I need all of that in my life, and because I understand that, I am able to actively seek it.

It is true that even though your spouse or partner doesn't have to check all, or even most, of the boxes on the list, there must be an underlying connection, maybe something you can't even put into words. There's a category I left off the list, because it's not important to everyone, but that's *faith*, and I think shared faith is so critical in fulfilling relationships. When I talk about faith, I don't necessarily mean a particular religion or set of religious beliefs, but I do mean a belief in something, something larger than us, something to keep you in awe of the miracle that we are even here in the first place.

Exercise 8.4

Do the hard thinking about what you are looking for in your relationships, where you derive strength, and what you need in order to be your best self. Ask yourself the deeper questions: What do you need? Force-rank the elements in the list above. Are there any others you can think of that are important to you? Write your own personal relationship mission statement: Who are you looking for in your life?

Exercise 8.5

Once you have the personal relationship mission statement, connect it to reality: Who fills these needs for you? Who might you want to lean on more? Who takes energy away from you, and doesn't fill some or all of your boxes? What are you missing, and where might you be able to find it?

Between how you spend your time and the people you spend it with, we've now covered the main elements of a Mission Driven life. What we haven't yet touched on are two final pieces: First, the ebbs and flows of a lifetime, and second, the mission itself, and how to find it, grow it, and truly change the world. Those are the subjects of the final two chapters.

CHAPTER NINE

Mission Driven Through the Stages of Life

When I arrived in Iraq, it was April, just a few months before the hot summer, where the daily high temperatures were already above 100 degrees and would soon sometimes reach into the 130s. I knew my team needed to be ready to work in the heat, so as we prepared all spring, I tried to push my team to do more. SEAL deployments overseas involve a lot of individual freedom. We choose how to stay fit, when and how to work out, and how to fill our time between missions. One (of many) homemade fitness devices we built was a humongous truck tire attached to a chain, attached to a weight belt that could be worn around the waist. We created a one-mile run and a "leaderboard" with everyone's times. Nothing drives SEALs more than competition—with self and with others. No one said anyone had to do that mile tire drag sprint in the heat, but those of us who did sure talked trash to the guys who didn't.

The activity was also metaphorical. The extra weight represented the heat to come, the drag we would all feel on our bodies. We would have competitions, and at the start of training, even though I was a decade older than many of the SEALs I was leading, I would win. "You are the guys fresh out of training," I would tell them. "Why am I the fastest one here?"

I was the fastest in part because I had been doing this the longest—intense training, focused on almost nothing else but my body and the mission, putting myself in the best possible position to outlast the enemy, to spot them from farther away, to react more quickly, to gain every advantage I could. We work out so we will see and respond to the enemy first—that's the goal. When life and death depend on whether you can drag a tire for a mile, your body figures out how to do it faster and faster and faster, while at the same time keeping your eyes up and out on the horizon, training yourself to be as observant as possible for threats, no matter how personally miserable you are.

Once I called out the new guys about being slower than me, it was game-on. I was going back and forth with a young new SEAL named Will Pipkin on the leaderboard, each of us trying intensely to shave a second or two off our times to regain the top spot. As our six-month deployment came to a close, I was a bit demoralized because Will was about ten seconds ahead of me—a nearly impossible time for me to overcome. But I decided I would go out by myself on the afternoon before we flew home. I gave it everything I had and then more. I did it—putting myself at the edge of human misery and perhaps never having done anything harder in my life. I overtook Will!

I decided I wouldn't tell him until we were on the plane home. We were all, of course, ecstatic to be going home, and when I gathered the regular tire-sprinters together, I prepared to have the last laugh. I told everyone about how I had crushed Will, how much better I was than him, how he just couldn't overcome the "old guy," etc. And Will, in a stone-cold emotionless response, said, "Sir—I knew you were going to do that. I planned for that. I got up at four a.m. and walked up to the leaderboard and saw your new time. About an hour ago, I beat you again by more than ten seconds."

All I could do was smile. How privileged I was to work with such great SEALs.

What's my larger point? If you dropped me in the desert right now and asked me to drag a truck tire for a mile, I would come in last or close to it—because that simply isn't my mission anymore. Life changes. And so if you think you can do the exercises in this book once and then you'll have it all figured out forever, you're absolutely wrong. Part of a Mission Driven life is understanding that the mission evolves and adapts, just as we evolve and adapt as individuals.

Chapter 6 was about the marginal incremental value of every choice in the moment; this chapter is about how the best choices can change over time. Let's return to the dilemma I posed earlier in the book: Spend a few precious hours perfecting a PowerPoint presentation, or take a walk with a friend? You may recall there is no right or wrong answer universally. It depends on the situation, on your priorities, and on the specifics. We can decide to spend those extra hours on a PowerPoint deck when we're twenty-three and need to impress our boss, but the equation may be different when we're fifty-three and trust that we've done enough and will get plenty more value from a walk with a friend.

Or perhaps not. It depends, as every decision does. Every moment of our lives is a choice, every instant a potential transition where we could decide to continue on the course we're on, or shift to something new and different. We will all shift many times throughout our lives—perhaps especially if families and children become part of our journey. Think back to Madeleine Albright and her story. She was at home with her kids until she was nearly forty. And that's okay—maybe even better than okay. Our priorities can shift by choice or by external circumstances that define them for us. But life isn't about having the same priorities over time. We can stagger the rewards and find our mission at every stage even if the balance changes over the years.

Life is ultimately a dynamic equation. You never know when you are going to need or want to make a shift. Circumstances change. And it takes all the meta-skills discussed earlier to navigate those changes, particularly resilience, and the ability to see hard days not as failures but as the moments most necessary for growth. Failures that lead to learning are successes in the end. Hard days that lead to easier ones make the pain worthwhile. It's never too late to make a better choice.

I've had so many near-death experiences. I still remember being in my Afghanistan makeshift office, on a video call with my wife and daughter, when the roof and walls shook from a rocket explosion. In those moments when you legitimately know it may all be over, you don't think of yourself. You think of who you're leaving behind. No one ever wishes from their deathbed that they had spent less time with the ones they love and more time at work. You can't take your money with you when you go. I was in Iraq and Afghanistan when improvised explosive devices (IEDs) were blowing up vehicles daily. Some days losses were counted in the dozens. Some of those IEDs contained 100+ pounds of explosives and were regularly going off, creating giant holes in the road. There was potential disaster lurking at every turn (and on the straightaways, too!). Each time I got into an armored vehicle, I wondered, *Would I even know if I died?*

All the clichés are true. You see your life flash before your eyes; you go back to your poorest choices and wish you could have done better. You go to the things you haven't done but want to. Honestly, that's one of the things that caused me to write *Never Enough*. It's not that I thought, *Oh no, I didn't write my book*. Rather, I realized, *I've been so privileged to live through and grow through so many situations that few ever do, for good and bad, that I feel I have to share, inspire, and help individuals and our nation*. And that's what drove me to write *Mission Driven* as well.

I know what patriotism is, and all I want in this life is to be known as an American and a patriot. Life is about making others and our great nation better. You *can* do better. *We* can do better. Every single moment of every single day.

Exercise 9.1

Think about what lingers for you, what you'd wish for if right now I told you—in thirty seconds you're going to be vaporized. It's a grim thought, but trust me, from experience, it helps clarify your thinking. Life will be over; the clock starts now. What do you think, what do you see, what do you want to say, and what do you wish you'd have done? Those things, maybe more than anything else, should be part of that success definition way back in chapter 2. Those things are your *who*, your mission, the North Star you should be aiming for.

But they don't all have to be achieved at once.

At every stage of the long game, we're making short game choices. The hope is that over time, we can fill all of our buckets, and power through every mission. We have to recognize that we can shift over days, months, years, and decades and that our mission is about more than just today—it's about an entire lifetime. I used to think only about taking the hardest job, and building the best foundation I could. Now I have a wider lens on things: I don't know where the future will take me, but I know that it's about more than just the hardest job. Instead, it's about the greatest impact without closing any doors for the future.

I talk to senior leaders whose needs have changed in even greater ways. As they look to their legacy, they are thinking not just about the greatest impact they themselves can make, but the impacts of the people they are training in the next generation and in the generations to come. They are also grappling with whether they have the energy and the desire to keep working as hard as they have for years or whether they would rather move into roles that give them more flexibility in other areas of their life. It is a constant balancing act, a recalibration based on changing feelings.

We don't necessarily feel Mission Driven at every moment, but we can craft a life that works for us as our needs and wants evolve, and feel like we're always pushing forward in at least some domains, even if we can't have it all.

SACRIFICING NOW FOR LATER AND LATER FOR NOW

If you make a long-term decision, almost by definition you are sacrificing something in the short term. It's not exactly a zero-sum game, but there are going to be times when there are clear trade-offs. On one level, we can think about trade-offs from a purely financial perspective: We sacrifice now so that we have more money later, saving instead of spending, cooking instead of ordering takeout, living in a smaller house now so we can afford a nicer retirement in the future.

We can also think about trade-offs from a time perspective. Parents, for example, sometimes confuse quality and quantity. A parent might worry that taking on a one-year master's program means less time playing with their toddler for a year. That may be the case—but you also have to ask if the toddler will remember that or remember the better life that resulted from the greater opportunities their parent ended up with. What about the future flexibility that will allow the parent to spend more time with them later? Aside from time, how about giving the toddler lessons in the value of hard work, setting and achieving goals, and educational achievement? On the other hand, what about wanting the toddler to feel like they are the first priority, above all else, and postponing the degree for a year or two? There are no right or wrong answers. We can decide that the benefits later are worth the sacrifices today. Or we can decide they aren't. We just have to decide with intention.

One thing to think about is how to minimize the short-term burdens so you can put as much energy as possible into the long game. You need to be as efficient as you can with the burdens you place on yourself. Imagine a scenario where you love warm weather and bigger backyards, and you hate snow and city living. You've decided in the long term you want to live in Florida, but the career opportunities are better right now in New York. You are accepting a weather and location burden right now, hoping it will create flexibility later that will allow you to move.

I like to think about burdens and sacrifices using what I call the backpack analogy. Every sacrifice we make gets carried by us in a backpack that grows heavier the more burdened we feel. The more we're carrying, the slower we move, and the fewer additional burdens we can take on. So if you're making sacrifices—like weather, location, money, or time—you have to ask yourself if you can find other ways to lighten the load.

We need to think about three things: (1) the weights we're putting in; (2) our ability to carry those weights; and (3) the weights we can take out. We also need to decide what's actually a weight. It may be that we can reframe some weights—commuting time, as one easy example—as positives. You might initially think of your commute as a burden, but what if you used your commute as time for learning through podcasts or audiobooks, phone calls to build relationships, meditation, writing a book (!), or any of a number of things that could mitigate what at first seems like a negative?

More broadly, we can often shift weights around in ways that aren't immediately obvious, especially if we pull back and look at how we might be able to frame the issue. If you're looking at a job that will have a lot of travel, for instance, and you don't want to be away from home so much—can you look at every element of the equation and figure out some possible changes that aren't currently on the table? Could your family move? Could you homeschool your children and take them on the road with you? Could the job be more flexible? Is there another job out there that isn't currently on offer but you could generate through the right networking leads?

We also need to think about the backpacks other people are carrying—not just our own. Perhaps we are taking on weight, but it's saving our family from even more burdensome problems. I took on the weight of serving the nation, to hopefully lighten the load for the 330+ million Americans benefiting from my service. I saw that as a pretty good trade-off. My wife took on the weight of being a single mother for much of my career so that I could serve more broadly. Together, we saw that as a worthwhile trade—but the math is different for everyone. If you are sacrificing so others may benefit, that is something worth considering, especially if you can architect your life over time so that what you lost for some amount of time eventually comes back to benefit you. I sacrificed in terms of salary in order to serve as a SEAL, but the work expanded my ability to earn more money now.

Are there specific things you can do to lighten your burden? Take the Florida–New York trade-off just discussed. Could you negotiate extra weeks of vacation? Work remotely? Invest extra money in a heating system for your patio so the winters aren't so cold?

Just like when doing the exercises to find your *who*, it is important to separate your own feelings and sense of mission from society's influence. We all struggle with external validation—we want others to approve of what we are doing—but this can change over time as well. Job titles may feel important at age thirty in a way they don't at age sixty, if priorities shift to family, flexibility, or health. Or a job title may feel more important at age sixty, depending on your peer group, as you struggle with staying relevant and fear retirement and a possible loss of identity. Working parents have this issue. I have this issue. I wrestle with my own life: Am I doing the right thing?

There are pressures, but a lot of them are external. Spend more time with your kids. Spend more time at work. We can't do everything at once. The important part is to focus on your own needs, not necessarily conform to someone else's expectations, stated or unstated.

There is also value, of course, to intrinsic goals even at times when external identity isn't obvious. I have had to find ways to redirect my motivation at times now, when my mission is very different than when I was on the battlefield.

What works for you may not work for other people. We all approach these questions differently, as we have throughout the book. Trade-offs that you are okay with may not be okay for someone else. Just know what you're choosing.

HOW YOU BUILD OVER TIME

I have seen people leave the SEALs and become all kinds of things, expected and unexpected. A BUD/S classmate of mine, Steve, did five years as a SEAL and is now a pastor—a totally different calling. My friend and another inspirational former SEAL, Jimmy May, is building an organization called Beyond the Brotherhood, to help SEALs transition beyond service. (Check it out at beyondthebrotherhood.org.) He's also a father, sometimes posting "Dad drops" on LinkedIn about being the best he can be at *that* job, just as he was the best on the battlefield.

Each of them worried about their next steps. They weren't certain they were building effectively over time. We all worry—but if your attempts to extend and expand your mission over time feel like they're failing, it is worth looking closer at how you're approaching the journey. Failure can mean a number of possible things:

First, you haven't done the work to understand your *who*. If you are anchored in the *what* and not the *who*, you are setting yourself up to be let down. Of course, we will all have disappointments, but if you stay focused on *who* you are, even if the external markers of success don't arrive, you can still take pride in the fundamental attributes of you and your endeavors. Yes, it can be unsatisfying if you don't clearly see the reward, but the only way to make the long game work is through persistence, determination, and grit. Go back and look at your *who* and really make sure it's right—not a crutch, but something continually worth striving for, a mission you're driven to achieve.

You can fail at the *what* but still be the *who* you want to be. I see it all the time where people may be erroneously seen as "failures" on external success metrics but have succeeded profoundly. My SEAL buddy Will Branum has publicly talked about his struggles transitioning out of the military. He had a long journey to find his next act, down into the deepest depths of wondering what to do with his life, and what his mission was. A lot of people would look at that as wasted time, but time is never wasted if you land somewhere great in the end. He has now dedicated himself to helping others be the best they can be, including recovering from their own combat traumas. Some could have seen his struggles and quickly dismissed him, but anyone looking at the big picture would see his successes, his mindset, and his ability to help and support others—and call it a victory. He is successful not because of a title or money or fame but because he really does have a mission and knows how he wants to move the world.

I was deeply shaken when my former teammate Jason Redman wrote in his first book, *The Trident*, that he felt like a failure and had a gun in his mouth as he contemplated suicide. I had no idea. That of course made me and others ask ourselves what else we're missing. It's truly scary when combat teammates who seem perfectly fine turn out not to be. Now Jason has become a supremely inspirational speaker, recently placing first out of sixty throusand entrants in a national speaking contest. He has created the Overcome Army, a collection of people who help each other be more positive and find the conviction they need to succeed in their lives. He nearly died on the battlefield, and then again back at home, and now he is inspiring so many with self-discipline and positivity (Google him for so much more). He found his *who* and it's awe-inspiring as he has changed countless lives.

Second, what if you are achieving the *whats*, but they haven't brought you the happiness and fulfillment you anticipated? This is big. External validation, as tempting as it can be to chase, doesn't get you to fundamental satisfaction. You may need to do a deeper analysis—what is the foundational problem here? Be objective and reflective; think about how much of your frustration is about you and how much is due to the universe and forces out of your control. Understand that failure is almost always traceable back to you—you have agency over your life!

If something isn't working for you, take ownership, and don't just throw up your hands. What could you be doing differently? Are you talking to the right people, and do you have the right exposure? Start from the orientation of understanding how and where you might be wrong. If you're convinced you have the right *who*, then ask yourself if there are other ways to achieve the thing you're chasing.

As an example: I was brought into VMware with an understanding I was going to spend some time proving my value, effectively acting as the chief operating officer, and then be given the title of COO once it was clear to everyone that I was contributing. That's not exactly what ended up happening. The CEO who brought me in, Pat Gelsinger, mentioned earlier, left to lead Intel after I'd been at the company for just three months. With Pat gone, the understanding that I had been hired to become COO was still in place, but my champion had left and there was no particular urgency to change my title. On the one hand, the name of my job didn't matter: I didn't care about the official role as long as I was having an impact, and I didn't need the title for my own ego. On the other hand, the COO title would unlock a different set of future opportunities, with the chance to have an even bigger impact at the next place I landed. So I did want the title changed to reflect the job, and I felt I had earned it with the work I had done since arriving.

I could have let things unfold on their own, trusting that my effort would be noticed. But I thought about my larger mission, and making sure I was in the best position to make the most impact going forward. I ended up stepping out of my comfort zone and advocating for myself, forcing the issue and pushing for the title change. It worked. It was an uncomfortable place to be—I am world-class at advocating for others and one of the world's worst at advocating for myself—but I reminded myself that I had agency, and I needed to do something or I'd start to become resentful.

Do we want to live in a world where titles matter? I don't. I want to live in a world where impact is all that counts. But the reality is that to make a certain kind of impact, sometimes you need the title. Sometimes you get to a point in your career where you need external validation to move the largest mountains. And sometimes you don't. It all depends on the situation. And it often changes over time.

In the final chapter, we look at how to think big and truly make the greatest impact possible. By being Mission Driven, it is not an overstatement to say you can change the world.

CHAPTER TEN

Mission Driven to Change the World

In the corporate arena, there is a scoreboard: stock price, revenue growth, net profit, a person's own salary—a number, perhaps flawed, against which people can judge their value. But feeling valued—and feeling like what you are doing has value to your community and to the world—is about so much more than a number. We all have to ask ourselves the questions: *Are we having the kind of impact we want? Is our mission the right one?*

The answers may be different for everyone, since we all have different goals and different measures, but the questions are the same. You should never be spending your time pursuing a mission where you don't see the ultimate value, whether that value is lifting up billions of others through an issue you care deeply about or giving you the financial flexibility to live the life you want.

Having a purpose when you're a SEAL is easy; the impact is often quite clear, life-and-death, solving very tangible problems around the globe. But finding purpose when it isn't quite so obvious can be more challenging. I've said already that being a SEAL, or serving in the military more broadly, is just one type of service, and we should all be serving in the way that makes the most sense for us, whether it's through a structured organization or not. The important part isn't what you do but that you do *something*, or lots of somethings, but in all cases get off the sidelines and take ownership of some small piece of this great nation and planet.

We all have to remember that everything is steered by someone, and so we just need to be one of those someones steering society in the direction we want it to move. The world can't just be made up of takers—people responding to decisions and events. Someone is causing those events, actions, and reactions, and there's no reason it shouldn't be you, me, all of us.

In the SEALs, we say a person dies two deaths. One is the physical, and the other is the last time anyone on earth says their name. I personally work really hard to #neverforget to keep my great teammates, in some small way, alive. That's why I've mentioned so many by name in this book, and why I talk about them whenever I can. *Who will keep your name alive when you're gone?* Just like the way John Connors impacted me without my ever meeting him, who are you impacting, who you may never meet?

In that spirit, Marcus Capone, Matt Roberts, DJ Shipley. Hardcore SEALs who contributed to mission after mission in Iraq with me on SEAL Team TEN. They have each wrestled with mental health challenges and the aftereffects of combat and, in fact, made a movie about it—*In Waves and War*, about Marcus struggling with PTSD after returning from Afghanistan and finding hope in psychedelic therapy. Marcus started a worthy nonprofit, Veterans Exploring Treatment Solutions (VETS), to help others access safe psychedelic therapy as well, in an extraordinary mission to end veteran suicide. In the SEALs, we had a clear no-drug policy and it has never been something I've needed or that has interested me, but I am now very grateful for people like Marcus looking for solutions to help people who are struggling. He is having great impact, and that impact will live on beyond the people he is able to physically help by himself.

WHAT IS YOUR SCOREBOARD FOR IMPACT?

Everyone's scoreboard is different. You need constant revising and checking in with yourself to be sure your scoreboard still makes sense. And sometimes you might still be missing something. I think about a group of people who support the SEALs, in a role that doesn't sound glamorous on first reflection. I'm talking about the procurement community, a bunch of great people serving on every major staff in the military, career civil servants who order and buy all the uniforms, body armor, guns, radios, everything the SEALs need to be successful. They are underloved and underappreciated, but their job is, of course, critical. We needed our supplies out there. And we needed people who could work within a budget and negotiate for the best deals on quality gear so that money could be spent on everything else that is needed in training and for the deployments and missions overseas.

I got a message on LinkedIn not long ago from someone in procurement at Special Operations Command (SOCOM) headquarters in Tampa, Florida, telling me she read *Never Enough* and got a lot

from the book, recommended it to others, and was just wondering…
Every year all the procurement leaders across SOCOM meet for a conference in Virginia Beach, 300 people, and she expected I was busy but
thought she'd ask if I would be willing to be the guest speaker.

I'll be honest that when I got her message, my instinct was to
politely decline. I get way more requests than I can consider. When I
get asked about an event, I go through my own force-rank analysis.
I can only do so many talks, but the talks are one of the ways I generate money to pay off mortgages for Gold Star widows and families,
so it's an unapologetically capitalist calculation. If it's in my back-
yard, that's one thing—but to get on an airplane and lose a day of
work, it's hard to justify if the money isn't there.

But I decided to call her after such a lovely note and decline in
a conversation rather than just sending an email. "I know you're
busy," she said, "and it was a long shot to reach out. I mean, it would
have been exciting for us, but—"

And as she was talking, I thought to myself—my calculation was
wrong this time, because what greater impact can I have than finding a
way to thank and motivate these people who devote their lives to making our Special Operations forces better? How awesome had it been to
read her note of appreciation for what I've done, and know that I am
exponentially more appreciative of what she and everyone else in her
role did for me and all of my teams over my entire SEAL career?

I told her I'd do it (for free, of course), and I figured I could see
some friends while I was down there, too—I lived in Virginia Beach
for thirteen of my twenty years of service. I flew in and didn't pay a lot
of attention to the arrangements in advance. I found myself in a taxi
heading down very familiar streets. I knew I was going to a Marriott

hotel, where the conference was, and where I'd be staying, but in my mind it was the one on the oceanfront in Virginia Beach—there's a whole stretch of hotels on the water. But we were headed to a hotel on the opposite side, on the bay, maybe 700 yards from where I used to live. I used to know the owners of the hotel, our daughters swam together, and we attended birthday parties together back when it was a family business, before they sold it to Marriott. My most powerful memory of the place was that my SEAL teammate and very close friend Kyle Milliken had his wedding reception there in 2008. Kyle was tragically killed in action in 2017 on a mission in Somalia after a fifteen-year career. It was supposed to be his last combat mission before heading to business school at the College of William & Mary, for which I had written his letter of recommendation, and where he had already been accepted. He was thirty-eight years old and left behind a beautiful family—his wife, Erin, and two children.

I got out of the taxi and was overwhelmed. How was I here? How was Kyle gone? I walked over to the spot where I knew I had taken a picture at his reception. How did I remember? Just a few days earlier, another friend had texted me that very picture, just to say he was thinking of me. I pulled up the picture on my phone. There were eight of us in the shot. Out of the eight of us, three were dead, two had been badly injured, and only three of us were still physically in one piece. I prayed for a moment, silently. I thought about Kyle and how much I missed him, and how I could use my talk to celebrate him and his life of service to this country.

"I do a lot of these talks," I told the audience that evening. "I push *Never Enough* without shame because it's not only a mission to help the reader and nation, but the profits go to charity and to date

I've paid off nine homes for Gold Star widows and their families. I do these things for pay, but I came down here for free because I want to say thank you. In 2008, I stood thirty feet from here"—I pointed to the exact spot—"and took a picture. There were eight of us drunk smiling SEALs in the frame, and three of them aren't here anymore, killed in action. It's heartbreaking, but the reason the rest of us made it through is because of you. Each and all of you. You bought us our guns and body armor; you bought us our radios, our uniforms, our night vision, our lasers, and everything that gives us our combat advantage. We take it all for granted. We never get to meet you. It's now a decade-plus since my last combat mission, but it's never too late to say thank you. Thank you for what you did to keep me alive, to keep my friends alive, to keep this country alive."

I made it real for them, or at least that's what I tried to do. Their work was not in vain. These were the people who get called the geeks, the bean counters, the paper pushers, etc. They are never seen. But those of us who know truly knew. Their efforts had real consequences, and one of those consequences was that I was able to stand up there in the front of that room and say thank you.

Who can you thank?

And what are you doing that people can thank *you* for?

There are a few final exercises to tackle as we finish this journey and bring all the work we've done throughout this book to bear.

Exercise 10.1

A retrospective reflection: Think about where you have landed to date. Map your life. Literally, take a piece of paper, turn it the long way, and draw the graph, birth to now. Where were the peaks and where were the dips, in any respect you choose to focus on? How did you handle the dips? What got you through to the other side? A high school friend of mine used to say, "Don't just float through life; make waves."

There are people who get through hard times by going inward, focusing on the kinds of things that make them happy: family, hobbies, friends. And there are those of us who go outward, trying to reach more people, make new connections, "network" like never before.

These are simply two different approaches, neither one right or wrong, and they tell you something about yourself. They tell you where your heart lies, what gives you the ultimate energy and strength.

Look hard at what got you through those high and low points in your life, and lean into that. Those patterns illustrate how you will get through tomorrow's highs and lows. Use the past to help the future. Learn how you recharge and recover, how you cope with disappointment, and the tools you've used in the past to redirect when your path heads off course. Hopefully at this point I've given you some new tools: intentionality, a meta-plan, the forced-rank lists of the attributes that matter to you, and a laser focus on what success really means and the *who* you are looking to be.

Exercise 10.2

Once you have finished looking back, look ahead: Are you, right now, anchored on where you are going, and do you have a handle on what's missing as you try to get there? Go all the way back to your *who*. After you've completed a book's worth of thinking and reflecting, does it still feel right? Is it still *who* you want to be? What's keeping you from getting there? And what would give you increasing confidence that you can make it? What are you doing—now, every day, every week, every month, every year—to push you closer? The question isn't rhetorical. Make a list. Write down how you're improving yourself, building your meta-skills, taking steps to achieve your mission.

Next, make a long-term plan. We both know it's going to be wrong. No one can predict the twists and turns. But if you were gaming it out, right now, what would it look like? If there is no reasonable path to the goal, then something's wrong. You either aren't thinking hard enough, or the goal is wrong. If any of the steps along the way feel unrealistic, push on that feeling. Why are the steps unrealistic, and what can you do to make them more likely to happen?

If you can plot one path, then almost certainly there are many possible paths to get there, paths you aren't yet able to see. Your meta-plan will help guide you, but for now, keep that one path in mind, and keep thinking about what you're doing—every day—to move 1% closer to where you desire.

WE CHANGE THE WORLD ONE STEP AT A TIME

A lot of the exercises in this book have been about future planning, or at least giving yourself a framework to plan, even as we know plans always—*always*—change. I do think it's also important to keep reminding ourselves that it isn't just about the future, but that what we do at every step along the way matters. It is not that you can't enjoy the journey—in fact, I'd make the case that you must enjoy the journey, or you're wasting the precious time you have on this planet. It's just that you must be striving at every step along the way if you're ever going to make progress.

The learning you get from the act of doing, every single day, has to be there. We all have the ability to make an impact right now—reaching out to a friend, lifting up a neighbor, a colleague, a stranger—and so no matter where you are going, there are things you can do today to have a positive impact. Whether or not you reach the big goals you set, you should always be setting small ones along the way. And if you do reach those big goals? You set another goal, an even bigger goal. There is never a mythical end state where angels come out and sing.

Exercise 10.3

Ask yourself this: If someone told you that you would never reach the ultimate expression of your *who*—that success, however you define it, was never going to happen—what would you do the same, day to day, and what would you do differently? To put it more concretely, if you knew you were never going to get a promotion, never find a new job, never make any more money than you are making right now, what would you change about your life?

The best answer is "nothing" because that means you're doing everything right. But, of course, we all make mistakes. If there are things that would be different, why can't you do those things right now, since we never know what the end state is going to be? Just like those near-death experiences I lived through—how can you make sure you're living with no regrets?

Exercise 10.4

Along the same lines, if you knew you *were* going to get everything you've ever imagined—more money, more security, more impact—no matter what you did each day, how would you live your life? Who would you want to help? How would you want to help them? And once again, what's stopping you from doing those things today?

Both sets of questions are the same, in case you didn't realize. Whether or not you're going to reach any particular end state, live your best life right now. Be Mission Driven in the long run, but in the short run as well.

This ability to embrace *now* while balancing today with the future is what separates being Mission Driven from garden-variety ambition. People think of ambition as a hunger for more—and while there's nothing wrong with having that hunger, you can't let it consume the opportunity to make a difference today.

You shouldn't hoard all your resources for a better tomorrow, because you don't know what tomorrow will bring, and you will miss out on all the impact you can make on the world that you're actually living in.

* * *

So how do you change the world?

Ask yourself not just what *you* need, but what the nation needs.

First, it needs you to be fulfilled and operating at your best, because we are strongest when everyone is strong. It needs you to be constantly getting better. It's not enough to stand on the sidelines and see a problem. If you see one, take action, whether that's organizing others around a common goal or taking a step to resolve the problem, big or small. I sometimes say we need AmeriCANs not AmeriCAN'Ts—and if that catches on, maybe I'll make it into a T-shirt.

This isn't a trivial point. When we are stressed—about work, about health, about family, about anything—our ability to look beyond ourselves is limited. We are less able to invest in other people, to help individuals, our community, the nation. We end up focusing on our own pile, and only once that's settled are we able to help others. How do we get over that anxiety? Partly it's with the kind of thoughtful planning this book is all about, but partly it's by understanding that our stress may not be so bad compared to others. Think about everyone bagging up their problems and throwing that bag into the middle of a room. Would you want your bag back, or someone else's? If you'd choose someone else's, think about why. What are you missing? More likely, you'd choose your own—and that should make you grateful that your problems aren't worse. Still, stress exists, and the more you can vanquish it, the better.

A dear friend of mine jokes about how he might have lost more shareholder value than any other CEO in history (not his fault—the forces at play at the time went far beyond him). But worse than the stress of watching his company lose billions of dollars? An unhappy personal life. He spent a number of years in a relationship that he only realized afterward had been making him miserable—and keeping him from extending beyond himself and reaching his potential. After the relationship ended, he was surprised to find how much better he felt, even at work. He was carrying so much pressure and stress within him, and until he let go of it, he could not achieve his full mission. His advice to others now is that you might not think the world can see your stress and pressure, but it can. When you become more carefree, confident, and happy, that makes it even easier for great things to find you.

Once you let the negative feelings go, you start presenting a different aura to the world. People want to be around others who seem successful, fulfilled, and at peace. They want to surround themselves with other Mission Driven individuals. And then, together, you can move the needle on important issues.

The second thing the nation needs is time and energy. It's basic logic: The more people using their time and energy to help the world, the better the world will become. Of course, time is finite, as are both mental and physical energy. The amount of energy you are devoting to your own craft and your own situation is energy you can't invest in others. But you need free energy to make an impact. You need space to invest in others. You see it in good leaders—they mentor, they teach, they help—and you see the inverse in bad leaders, who are only looking for excuses to say "no." How do you free up that space? Invest in things that give you energy.

Exercise 10.5

What gives you energy? It's different for everyone, but you can make a list: talking to a friend, taking a walk, exercising, eating well, putting down your phone, reading a book, painting a picture, jamming on your guitar—the options are endless.

The third thing the nation needs is your unique ideas and gifts. Your stamp on others, helping to create future leaders who will do even more for the world in the generations to come. We don't teach people how to be effective mentors, but we should. Bad mentors talk about themselves. Good mentors don't make assumptions that they know someone else's goals or mission. (And—it should be no secret by now—that's the whole premise of *Mission Driven*. I don't have your mission. I just want to help you find yours and to achieve it, both for yourself and for the nation.)

First, figure out who to mentor—a step most people ignore, but we can't mentor everyone, so find people in whose lives you think you can make a difference. Then, understand your mentee's goals, and help sharpen their conviction around them. Help them understand what they want to be doing and why. Don't assume they have the same strengths as you do, or the same challenges. Think about who can use their help, and what you can do to maximize their impact, now and in the future. What would change their life?

And in the process of helping them, you will almost certainly feel rewarded as well. Just like visiting wounded warriors made us more energized than when we walked in, feeling completely in awe of how this country has people who sacrificed so much but still have a positive attitude, it's the same thing with mentoring. To be around someone who is first figuring out how to unlock their potential is invigorating. And there are always lessons that emerge from seeing how someone else's mind works, and how someone else uses their innate gifts.

That's all the nation needs. You, at your best, with time and energy to give your unique ideas and gifts. Your mission—in fact, everyone's mission—is to bring your best to the table every single day, working intentionally toward lifting up your own life and the lives of those around you. Doing the work to clarify that mission and put it into action is how you become Mission Driven and live a Mission Driven life.

Writing *Never Enough* allowed me to scale myself beyond the individual conversations I'd often have when people asked me to talk to their kids who were thinking about joining the SEALs and explain what that life was like. Similarly, I hope this book lets me help everyone I can't reach one-on-one as they try to achieve a more rewarding life for themselves, no matter the domain in which they work.

Throughout my work on *Never Enough* and again on *Mission Driven*, I've had to keep reminding myself of the ultimate goal, and why I'm doing this. I've had to understand my own mission and keep it close to me every step along the way. As I said in the introduction, I'm doing this for Gold Star families, to pay off mortgages for the spouses and children of my brave teammates who died for our country. And by doing so, I'm helping them to better achieve their own missions, freeing them from worrying about how they are going to pay their bills so that they can help others, people I will never meet, people who may never understand the chain of impact that is making possible the help they're getting.

It all reminds me of a note I got from one of the Gold Star widows whose mortgages I was able to pay off. Her husband was a heroic SEAL who completed three deployments and ultimately lost his life to PTSD, traumatic brain injury, and a degenerative neurological condition caused by repeated head trauma from the blast exposure he experienced at war. Piles of awards and decorations couldn't save him from succumbing to the injuries he suffered, and I felt so privileged to be able to relieve some of the burden his wife and children felt after his passing. His widow wrote to me:

I find it difficult to capture the ethereal emotions of the heart when it has been given such an incredible gift. How do you capture in words what [paying off our mortgage] means for a family? We bought this house in 2001, not long after we were married and just weeks after the terrorist attacks altered our lives in ways we couldn't even imagine. As he went off to Afghanistan for the first time, I began to make this little place our home. We got a dog, made friends with the neighbors, hosted dinner parties, all in between his unending cycles of workups and combat deployments. This was home; this was shelter, safety and love. This is where in 2005 we brought home our firstborn... where we introduced her to her brother, in 2008, and learned quickly that two kids are exponentially harder than one.

This house is where in 2005 and 2011 we cried together over the extraordinary loss of so many friends at once; and where we celebrated the arrivals of so many perfect new lives in the births of our friends' children.

It's where we made dinner, had impromptu family dance parties, got ready for school and work, nursed colds and fevers, and undertook a thousand different activities that make up a life. This was sanctuary. This was HOME....

You have erased a fear that [my kids] have been carrying for nearly eight years now....

A few weeks before we talked, I had hit a stumbling point. I was sad and lonely, worried about finances, and having an extended pity party. I was considering a job offer that, while it would pay well, would have left me empty and unable to do the things about which I was passionate—helping others. I was feeling bitter, jealous and angry....

Your gift was a miracle!

I now have less worry about finances and can hold tight to the physical embodiment of our family love and spirit. But we also now have the opportunity that financial stability provides to send our light, our gratitude and our hope into the world in real and meaningful ways.

I can continue to help military families and make a difference....

[My kids] have an added layer of security, so they can focus more on their talents and strengths that will enrich the world....

We endured burning. But I promise that every day moving forward we will shine our collective light into the world so that your gift continues to give.

I can't help but tear up every time I read that.

That note was in my mind every step along the way as I wrote this book. By focusing on my mission, I'm enabling her to focus on hers, and keep her job at an organization that helps the SEAL community she feels so connected to—a job that may not pay all that well but allows her to help the people she cares about. Those people will pay the help forward. And the people they help will pay it forward as well. That is the magic of being Mission Driven, and the magic I hope you can all find in your lives, no matter what your individual goals may be.

If this helped you, then I urge you to join the *Mission Driven* family. Pay it forward and help me have an impact on people that neither you nor I may ever have the chance to meet. And then go out and live your own mission, impact even more, and make the fulfilling life that you've been hoping for.

There's nothing this country and its amazing citizens—led by you, your unique mission, and all the people you touch along the way—can't achieve.

ACKNOWLEDGMENTS

I never aspired to write one book, let alone two. And I've learned that, just like in the SEALs, success simply doesn't happen without a great team.

First [as always], to Ni. You're my love and my life. Thank you for your continued support, guidance, wisdom, humor, and keeping me in check. However much you think I love you—it's infinitely more. Thank you for inspiring me and always being the example. Shoooterrrr!!!

Maeson. You will always be my little girl. I love you with all my heart! I've always seen how Mission Driven you are; you are an inspiration to me. A parent can have no greater joy than to see their child positively impact the world. I am proud not just of all you do, but for who you are. DLY. SAP. HW.

To my parents, Ted and Elizabeth Hayes. This book is another reflection of the values, character, and work ethic you instilled and inspired in me from my earliest days. Thank you for being you, for your lifelong unwavering support, and for all you have given me.

To my siblings, Jen, John, and Maryclare. Thank you for being awesome examples of Mission Driven from the beginning of our lives together and now with your own families. Thanks for being the incredible siblings, parents, aunts and uncle, inspirations, and best friends you each are.

To Bumpa. I miss you, but you live on in me. Thank you for teaching me selfless service, mission, meaning, and a life of purpose. Thank you for your stories of bravery, work ethic, character, charisma, and humor. Thank you for your service—from Pearl Harbor on that fateful day, to the war in Korea, and to Pax River test piloting the Navy's first helicopters. Thank you for your sword. Thank you for telling me not to die for my country, but to go on living for it.

To the greatest book team in the world. First, Jeremy Blachman. There's just no one better on the planet. You're a gift—and your gift is a gift to others. It's impossible to envision anyone better to brainstorm, think, and create with. Your thoughts and words are always so spot-on. I can't imagine a better teammate and friend.

Next, Gina Ruebensaal, my grad school classmate whose always-smart comments in the lecture hall quietly scared me into thinking I was an admissions mistake! I'm not sure I understood a word you said until our second year. Your early thoughts and brainstorming sessions formed such a foundation for *Mission Driven* and I'm eternally grateful.

Anthony Mattero—You're so much more than the world's best book agent. You're a giant inspiration, a never-ending fountain of wisdom, and your proactive, positive, and supportive orientation means more to me than you can know. Thank you for partnering again. No finer friend or teammate!

Dan Ambrosino—thank you for launching this project at Hachette. Your enthusiasm made this book possible. Amar Deol—thank you for stepping in and lifting *Mission Driven*. Your insights and energy have been invaluable. Thanks as well to Niyati Patel, Morgan Spehar, and the entire Hachette team.

To my brothers in the SEAL Teams. It's impossible to thank the hundreds of SEAL friends who have challenged me, taught me, and inspired me to be better every day. Thank you for the opportunity to serve and learn with and among you.

To my fallen teammates. I struggle without each of you. I think of you and your families almost every day. I live my life dedicated to your memories and legacies and the loved ones you left behind. I will never forget. I'm sorry. And at the same time, thank you. LLTB.

To you. Thank you for reading—and thus supporting Gold Star families. Just as important if not more, thank you for thinking about how you contribute to making our nation and our world better through your own unique ambitions, gifts, goals, and talents in the ways that make the most sense to YOU. Thank YOU for being Mission Driven!

ABOUT THE AUTHOR

MIKE HAYES is the former commanding officer of SEAL Team TWO, leading a two-thousand-person Special Operations task force in southeastern Afghanistan. In addition to a twenty-year career as a SEAL, Mike was a White House Fellow, served two years as Director of Defense Policy and Strategy at the National Security Council, and has worked directly with both Presidents George W. Bush and Barack Obama. Beyond his military and government service, Mike is the founding board member of the National Medal of Honor Museum in Arlington, Texas, and he started his own 501(c)(3), The 1162 Foundation, which has paid off twelve Gold Star widows' mortgages to date. In the private sector, Mike has served in several C-level roles and is currently Managing Director at Insight Partners, a software investment firm with $90 billion of regulatory assets under management and 600+ portfolio companies. He lives in Sunapee, New Hampshire, and Westport, Connecticut, with his wife and daughter.

Author Mike Hayes donates 100 percent of his profits from *Mission Driven* to The 1162 Foundation, a 501(c)(3) he founded that pays off mortgages for Gold Star families. Mike, like all SEALs of his era, has buried more than seventy teammates. His mission now is to help the surviving spouses and children of service members who have been killed in action or who died by suicide. Recognizing and thanking these families that continue to pay the ultimate sacrifice every single day helps them to stabilize and rebuild their lives.

At publication, The 1162 Foundation has paid off twelve mortgages for Gold Star families—but there is so much more work to be done. Use the QR code below if you would like to join Mike on this mission and support the effort to help these incredible families.